The God We Worship

Adoring the One Who Pursues, Redeems, and Changes His People

EDITED BY

JONATHAN L. MASTER

D1466817

PUBLISHING

P.O. BOX 817 • PHILLIPSBURG • NEW JERSEY 08865-0817

Unless otherwise indicated, Scripture quotations are from *ESV Bible*® (*The Holy Bible, English Standard Version*®). Copyright © 2001 by Crossway Bibles, a publishing ministry of Good News Publishers. Used by permission. All rights reserved.

Scripture quotation marked (RSV) is from the *Revised Standard Version of the Bible*, ©1946, 1952, 1971 by the Division of Christian Education of the National Council of the Churches of Christ in the United States of America. Used by permission.

Scripture quotations marked (NIV) are from the *HOLY BIBLE, NEW INTERNATIONAL VERSION*®. NIV®. Copyright © 1973, 1978, 1984 by International Bible Society. Used by permission of Zondervan Publishing House. All rights reserved.

Scripture quotations marked (NKJV) are from *The Holy Bible, New King James Version*. Copyright © 1979, 1980, 1982, Thomas Nelson, Inc.

Scripture quotations marked (NRSV) are from the *New Revised Standard Version Bible*, copyright © 1989 the Division of Christian Education of the National Council of the Churches of Christ in the United States of America. Used by permission. All rights reserved.

Scripture quotation marked (NASB) is from the *NEW AMERICAN STANDARD BIBLE*®. ©Copyright The Lockman Foundation 1960, 1962, 1963, 1968, 1971, 1972, 1973, 1975, 1977. Used by permission.

Unless otherwise indicated, Scripture quotations in chapters 1, 2, and 10 are taken from the New International Version.

Italics within Scripture quotations indicate emphasis added.

Printed in the United States of America

Library of Congress Cataloging-in-Publication Data

Names: Master, Jonathan L., editor.
Title: The God we worship : adoring the one who pursues, redeems, and changes
  his people / edited by Jonathan L. Master.
Description: Phillipsburg : P&R Publishing, 2016.
Identifiers: LCCN 2015043795| ISBN 9781629952079 (pbk.) | ISBN
  9781629952086 (epub) | ISBN 9781629952093 (mobi)
Subjects: LCSH: God (Christianity)--Congresses. | God (Christianity)--Worship
  and love--Congresses. | Theology, Doctrinal--Congresses.
Classification: LCC BT103 .G6425 2016 | DDC 231.7--dc23
LC record available at http://lccn.loc.gov/2015043795

To Bob and Leslie Doll

Contents

Editor's Preface

IT IS AN HONOR to write a preface for a book such as the one you have in your hands, but for me the deeper privilege was to be able to hear these addresses as they were first given—in historic Princeton, on a succession of November weekends over ten years.

The Princeton Conference on Reformed Theology was founded by some Christian friends who had benefitted tremendously from the flagship Philadelphia Conference on Reformed Theology. Year after year, they saw the fruit borne by the faithful preaching and teaching in Philadelphia and wondered whether something on a smaller scale might be used by God in Princeton. While Princeton has a long tradition as a center of confessional Protestant theology, it is now known more for its quaint downtown and for the elite university that lies at its center.

These friends began to meet and earnestly pray, and they contacted the Alliance of Confessing Evangelicals to see if a regional conference might be possible. Thus was born the Princeton Conference. The Alliance hosts many regional conferences now, but Princeton was the pioneer. The working idea behind each conference was always the same: sound doctrine, preached. To hear these addresses—this sound doctrine—proclaimed in Princeton, and to engage in glorious singing and praying with those who were gathered, was a delight. But make no mistake: the venue was of far less importance than the content.

As I read over these selections, I cannot help but recall the occasions when they were first delivered. But, while they were given at a particular time to a particular audience, the reality is that these are timeless. All of these sermons explore and expound upon the nature of God—who he is, how he draws sinners to himself, how he is at work providentially, and how he is to be approached by us in worship. In a sense, the glory of these sermons is that they never begin with man as their subject. They are focused on the triune God revealed in the Bible: the Creator, the Redeemer, and the source of all that is true.

I remember one of the early prayer meetings, when preparations were being made for what would be the first or second Princeton conference. A plan was formed, even then, for future conferences. Each year's addresses would explore a different aspect of the God of the Bible. This planning decision was motivated by the understanding that the doctrine of God was like a brilliant diamond: its facets needed to be held up to the light continually, moving Christians to greater knowledge of God and to greater wonder. The intent was to host these events in such a way that students could attend as well—a multigenerational reflection on the majesty of God. In fact, although it was never verbalized in quite this way, I always thought of our efforts in terms of David's words in Psalm 145:

I will extol you, my God and King,
and bless your name forever and ever.
Every day I will bless you
and praise your name forever and ever.
Great is the LORD, and greatly to be praised,
and his greatness is unsearchable.

One generation shall commend your works to another,
and shall declare your mighty acts.

On the glorious splendor of your majesty,
    and on your wondrous works, I will meditate.
They shall speak of the might of your awesome deeds,
    and I will declare your greatness.
They shall pour forth the fame of your abundant goodness
    and shall sing aloud of your righteousness. (Ps. 145:1–7)

David includes all the elements that we prayed about during those early days of the conference: the need to bless God's name, the unsearchable greatness of his being, our desire for generations to commend God's works to one another, and the glorious singing that results from meditation on the goodness of God.

By God's grace, these things happened year after year in November. For some of us, the conference at Princeton became one of the spiritual highlights of the year. And the truths that were proclaimed—the sound doctrine contained in this volume—can sustain meditation on God's goodness even now.

The structure of this book is fairly simple. The addresses are not printed in the chronological order in which they were preached; instead, they are thematically presented. The book begins by meditating on the glory of God, then on the utter ruin of the fall of man. Then the call and responsibility to worship God is addressed, along with his sovereign providence, mercy, and grace in making sinners into worshipers. Finally, the sanctification of the believer, along with the absolute truth-claims of Jesus Christ, is presented. The book is essentially organized according to the revelation of our triune God, beginning with God the Creator and lawgiver and moving to the work of God in sending his Son, Jesus Christ. Finally, it ends by addressing the person of the Holy Spirit and the way in which the Spirit-inspired Word of God gives us thorough guidance in our understanding of the Lord.

Because these chapters began their life in a conference set-ting, it is only right that I thank some of those who served on the conference team. Many contributed, but special recognition needs to be extended to Ray and Micheline Watrous, Bran-don and Lynette Hull, Bob and Leslie Doll, Kathleen Hurley, and, more recently, Matt Ristuccia. Of course, much of the behind-the-scenes work—both in the conference and for the book that has resulted—was done by the Alliance of Confess-ing Evangelicals and its dedicated and capable staff. Speaking more personally, both Janet Master and Marissa Rumpf gave me significant assistance in transcribing and editing these sermons, which previously existed only as recordings.

Early printed programs for the conference would contain a message about the conference topic, written by the chair. For many years this was written by Ray Watrous, and he always ended, appropriately, with the Latin phrase translated "to God alone be the glory." Indeed, it is my prayer, and the prayer of all those involved in this project, that God alone receive the glory, as these addresses are continually read and as God's greatness is repeatedly extolled.

Jonathan L. Master

1

God's Glory Revealed

BRYAN CHAPELL

WE ALL HAVE some dates forever fixed in our memories: November 22, 1963, Dallas; Saigon at the end of Tet; September 11, 2001, New York. As we saw the headlines following those dates that seemed to make the world come apart, we wondered, "What is God doing? Can there ever be glory again in those places?"

In Isaiah 6, a similar tragedy has just occurred. Isaiah mentions the death of King Uzziah—an unsettling blow to the people of Judah. During his reign, Uzziah had kept the wheels of commerce spinning and the walls around the nation secure. Now that he has died, people are wondering whether the good times will continue, whether their place will still be secure. Into this uncertainty comes a word, not in headlines from a reporter, but from a prophet. Isaiah has interviewed the Most High God—and he says that things will come undone. It is not a word that the people want to hear, but with the word there is glory.

Perhaps you can sense the glory by considering another front page from some years ago. I don't remember the headline, but I do remember two front-page pictures. In the first, various foreign dignitaries were visiting the president at Reagan National Airport. Behind the president was Air Force One, and alongside were the rainbow colors of the flags of the nations. Although I dimly remember that picture, the glory on display was not memorable. After all, there had been too many summits of nations, too many pictures of presidents on parade. But there was a second, smaller picture on the same page. This shot showed a woman kissing an infant on the lips. The caption explained that she was the first American to adopt a child with AIDS. At that time, our nation did not understand the disease or its source, so people were terrified, responding more out of fear than of reason. Consider these two pictures: the president in great pomp, and a woman kissing a child, perhaps at great sacrifice to herself. Which was the greater glory?

Such a question is difficult to answer. After all, how is glory measured? But we of the Reformed faith have to answer. How can we say that man's chief end is to glorify God and enjoy him forever if we don't understand glory? How can we know our life's purpose if we do not recognize which is the greater glory? Perhaps we can understand as we see how God displays his own glory in Isaiah 6. His display of glory comes through an expression of his holiness: "In the year that King Uzziah died, I saw the Lord seated on a throne, high and exalted, and the train of his robe filled the temple" (6:1). The marks of his holiness are on display; God's sovereignty is on display. Even as the nation wonders, "Has everything come apart?" and God is seemingly gone, Isaiah goes into the temple and sees a throne. God remains so holy that his purity itself is radiant. In the face of this glory, the heavenly host cover themselves so as not to be exposed to the radiance of the holiness of God. Even the angels are unable to look upon this radiance so cauterizing, so clean, so exposing that it's deadly. So great is the effulgence of the glory of God that even the heavens cannot contain it; it rolls, as the train of his robe, down into the earth.

There is no parallel setting in Israel's history or experience. Thrones don't belong in temples. But as Isaiah walks into the temple, the heavens are opened and he sees God seated on his throne. What does this mean? The world may seem undone, but God is still on his throne. He still lives. He still rules. The episodic nature of our existence, good or bad—that which comes undone, that which seems to unravel—does not touch him. He is not undone by what undoes us. He is sovereign, shining in his glory. He is high and exalted. Only his robe comes down to the earthly temple. God himself remains apart, untouched by the worst things of this world, not sullied by earth's stain.

And if we are unable to perceive how great and magnificent is this mark of the holiness of God, the seraphim begin to give us some measure of the greatness of this glory as they sing, "Holy, holy, holy is the LORD Almighty; the whole earth is full of his glory" (v. 3). If the Hebrews wanted to emphasize something, they would double the expression. Here the angels triple the word, as if to say that the word cannot contain the measure of the holiness of God. It is beyond the degree that we can imagine, let alone express. Remember these words—"Holy, holy, holy is the LORD Almighty"—because they occur again in Revelation 4, where the angelic host is still singing before God. John there adds that they will sing that song as long as the Lamb sits upon the throne, and he will sit upon the throne forever.

God is the holy God of the Old Testament, he is the holy God of the New Testament, and he is the holy God of the new creation. He is the eternally holy God, holy beyond our estimation and holy beyond time. And because we cannot capture in our human finiteness what it means to see God in all his holiness, we actually have a drama enacted before us. God often expresses his glory in the Old Testament in storm, in lightning and thunder. When God descends to Mount Sinai, clouds surround the mountain. Lightning flashes and thunder roars. Now this storm is inside the temple.

Isaiah 6:4 records that "at the sound of [the angelic] voices the doorposts and thresholds shook and the temple was filled with smoke." Why smoke? The smoke comes from the altar of atonement, the place where Israel is supposed to offer sacrifice for sin. Now the smoke overflows the temple, as if to show how great would be the sacrifice needed to satisfy the holiness of God. The smoke forms a dense, black cloud, but in this dark cloud fly seraphim. Their name means "burning ones." Like flashes of incessant lightning they fly through the cloud, and, like the storm, their presence is audible. They thunder their song. These are not the sweet angelic strains of heaven that we often imagine. At the thunder of their "Holy, holy, holy is the Lord Almighty," the foundations of the temple, set in the core of the earth, shake so that earth itself is shaken.

The thunder of the holiness of God drives the prophet to his knees. Face down, he calls out, "Woe to me! . . . I am ruined!" (v. 5). The Old Testament word for "glory" means "weight." The revelation of the glory of God bears down even upon a holy man of God, so that his knees can no longer support him, and he is prostrate before God and cries out his own ruin.

At the 1996 Promise Keepers conference in Atlanta, Georgia, the nearly forty thousand clergy present were urged by the speaker to repeat antiphonally to one another these words from Isaiah 6. So forty thousand voices cried, "Holy, holy, holy is the Lord Almighty; the whole earth is full of his glory." When they said it to one another, men got out of their seats. Some got on their knees. Some fell on their faces, because you cannot receive the holiness of God without exposing your own sin, your utter unworthiness, and the necessity of worship. What should God's people understand when he reveals his holiness? Their unholiness. Even as the heavenly host seek to cover themselves, we recognize that we have no right to stand before such a God. The Creator of the universe is still enthroned, and he is holy.

The manifestation of God's holiness is meant to humble, to break, but also ultimately to restore. How does that happen? Once we recognize how great the holiness of God is, we recognize how awful our sin is. And when we recognize how awful our sin is, we can recognize how wonderful our salvation is. If God is not very holy, then our salvation is not very great. But if God is holy, then his ability to reveal that holiness to finite beings such as you and me, and yet to claim us as his own, means that the gospel is wondrous, amazing, glorious. So when we gather, we not only worship his glory but also desire that the whole world would know it as we do.

In my ministry, I proclaim the salvation of our God. There are times in the work of the church when I seem to be plowing on such dry ground that I wonder if it is worth it. We who minister seem so often to be torn up with our own internal debates and difficult enterprises, unable to agree on basic aspects of our mission to the world. When I fail, I am not the only one who is disappointed, yet God, who has every right to be disappointed in me, still calls me in his love. God, who always has every right to cast me on my face before him, has nonetheless shed the blood of his Son on my behalf, so that his holiness would be my holiness and his righteousness my own. And since this God, so glorious in his holiness, would call me his own child, I know that if I can share the greatness of his glory with another person, that is good.

Yes, his holiness is a great glory. But there is a still greater glory. Greater than the holiness transcendent is the holiness transferred—not merely the glory of holiness, but the glory of grace. Here is the prophet—undone. Verse 5 reads, "'Woe to me!' I cried. 'I am ruined! For I am a man of unclean lips.'" He knows he cannot join the angel's song. His unclean lips make him unworthy. Not only that, but he admits, "I live among a people of unclean lips, and my eyes have seen the King, the LORD Almighty."

Now we know why the prophet trembles. According to the Old Testament, a person could not see God and live. Yet Isaiah has seen God in all his glory. No one of mere human nature could now survive, and so God must change his nature—and in verse 6 he does: "Then one of the seraphs flew to me with a live coal in his hand, which he had taken with tongs from the altar. With it he touched my mouth and said, 'See, this has touched your lips; your guilt is taken away and your sin atoned for.'" Here the angel carries a burning coal from the altar, taken with tongs. Even the angel does not want to be burned by it. Yet that burning coal gives the sweet burning of a divine kiss to a wounded prophet. Here we see grace—grace in great glory.

What are the marks of that grace? The infinite becomes intimate. This great God in all his holiness, who could remain exalted, removed, and unmoved at the plight of the prophet, sends a messenger from heaven. Heaven itself reaches down and touches the sinner. This is a great glory because whenever the infinite becomes intimate, glory comes.

Just think of that in terms of one aspect of the glory of God: his omnipresence. A friend of mine, a student at Covenant Seminary some years ago, told me that he was once studying in the library, trying to fathom the omnipresence of God. He pored over all the verses, read the theologians, and was getting some idea of the omnipresence of God as he tried to comprehend intellectually what it meant that God is in all places at all times. But what struck him then was this: if God is omnipresent, then God was present with him in that library at that moment. God's omnipresence meant that the heavenly God of all creation had his hand on that young man's shoulder right then, just as he has on our shoulders right now. When the infinite becomes intimate, we realize that the greater glory is really great grace.

We see the measure of glory revealed also in the seraph's flight and the burning coal. In the temple there are many sacrifices, but though their smoke of atonement fills the temple, they are insufficient—for here we see the prophet prostrate, still facing his sin. We see that sin is still not fully atoned for, for the fire on the altar will not go out until a perfect Lamb is slain. All the sacrifices in the temple presage what has come, even the death of our Savior. In him, the infinite becomes intimate at the cost of the Son of God. The temple's sacrifices are not enough; grace must come, and its full measure comes when the purpose of this sacrifice is finally accomplished. God, at infinite cost to himself, makes you and me his own sons regardless. Such cost for such as we? What great glory!

Some years ago, I had a friend who told me about her family. Her father was a believer, but neither she nor her brother had accepted the faith. Her brother had gone off and was living a rather wild life, but one day he called, saying that he was coming home by train and wanted his father to pick him up. His dad offered to go down to the station after work, and one of his coworkers happened to go with him. The two men stood on the platform, waiting for the son to come off the train. Various people got off and walked past. In the midst of the crowd, a very large man got off with a great beard, flowing hair, cap turned sideways, and a flowing black cape. The business partner jabbed an elbow into the ribs of my friend's father and said, "Who would want to be the father of that?" Immediately the man went up to embrace his son in front of his partner. Here we see no pride, but a willingness to lay everything aside to show his son love.

Just so, God, the exalted, holy, untouched One, in the person of his Son, took on the sin of the world to embrace you and me. That's how great the cost was, and that's how great the glory is. Even the seraph declares the effect of this grace in verse 7: "See, this has touched your lips; your guilt is taken away and your sin atoned for." Here we see the cauterizing, purifying effect of the work of God. Our guilt is taken away, our sin is atoned for—covered, removed—and the price is paid, not by us, but by heaven.

Now this prophet, who has been prostrate before God, hears him ask, "Whom shall I send?" and, in regal Trinitarian voice, "Who will go for us?" (v. 8). And the prophet responds, "Here am I. Send me!" Not only has guilt been removed, but the heart has been restored. The one who felt that he could do nothing, who had no right even to stand, stands and says, "I will serve the Most High God." And what else does he call himself? Flipped around, "Here am I" is "Here I AM." This unworthy one—who should have no status, no standing, no justification at all to approach God—assumes a title of God, proclaiming, "Whatever you call me to do, I will do." Isn't that amazing? That is what grace is supposed to accomplish.

Even in our evangelical circles, it is easy to preach a half-gospel, the gospel of simply removing sin. But if God has only taken away your debt, you still have a zero-sum balance. God has done something more. He has given to us his glory, his holiness, his righteousness. We are not just those whose debt has been taken away; we are those who have the riches of heaven on our behalf, even the holiness of God transferred to us. We have his glory.

This transfer is the greatest glory. It is the wonder of the gospel, the beauty of our faith, that we stand before God not on our own merit, but on his merit. He who has such holiness and grandeur that we have no right to approach him, hardly any right to view him, as even the angels cannot gaze upon that holiness, nonetheless considers us as holy as he is by the grace of heaven. This grace is what inspires us. It is what lifts us in our mission and instills in us a longing to speak to the world. We have such glory, such great grace, that it makes our hearts warm for the things of God.

Not until I began to perceive that my holiness was not my own, but God's righteousness on my behalf, could I truly find joy. He does not count me worthy because I'm performing well enough to gain some of his holiness. Rather, I have realized that when I was totally unworthy, he transferred to me all of his righteousness, all of his holiness. When that glory fills me, I can step off the "performance treadmill" and stop trying to please God enough to make him love me. I can recognize the joy of being loved by God, not because of anything in me, but because of his mercy alone: "But when the kindness and love of God our Savior appeared, he saved us, not because of righteous things we had done, but because of his mercy" (Titus 3:4–5).

When I know that joy, I can begin to love lost people. I am now not seeking to convert them for my sake; I am not even seeking to convert them so that I can please God. The wonder of the love of God on my behalf is such great grace that the natural response of the regenerate heart is to share this grace with someone else: "Come, find the mercy of God that I have found. This is wonderful; this is great; this is glorious; this is good—not because I am better than you, not because I earned this in any way, but because God in his mercy has made me his own. Let me tell you about this gospel." Sharing God's love is now my joy and not my burden.

We are plowing in hard ground. Isaiah was told not only to deliver a message of judgment, but also that this message would be preached to a people whose hearts were hardened. Yet it became the passion and glory of his life to go out into this hard ground, because it was his purpose to glorify God and enjoy him forever. There is no greater joy to the regenerate heart than to say, "This holy God made me holy, through no work of mine, but through the love of my Savior!"

I asked earlier which picture reveals the greater glory: the picture of parading presidents or the picture of a mother taking a diseased child into her heart and life. Perhaps the greatest glory would be if the president were to kiss the sick child—not likely. But something even greater than this mother's love has happened. We have found the greatest glory in the pages of the Word of God, where the King of heaven in the person of his Son came to touch diseased children like you and me, taking our sickness upon himself, so that he would die and, through the glory of that great act, we would be raised from death and live forever. This is the greatest glory: that a holy God would be so gracious. Let it be our life's highest joy to let the world know of this great glory.

2

Called by God to Worship

ONE DAY, AS I was walking down Broadway in New York City, a woman approached me. She was, I guess, in her early thirties and seemed frantic. She asked if I could help her out with some money to buy diapers for her baby, mentioning as she talked that she was rushing off to a job interview. When I looked into my wallet (recognizing her two "lines" for what they were), to my dismay I found that I had only twenty-dollar bills. I was stuck. There I was, standing before this woman with my wallet wide open. And, after all, I did want to help her out. So I pulled out twenty dollars and gave it to her. Then an extraordinary thing happened, the sort of thing that doesn't happen much in New York: the woman burst into tears, threw her arms around me, and said, "Thank you, thank you." I didn't know what to do. All I could find to say was, "God bless . . . God bless," before I went on my way.

I don't tell this story because I want to prove what an extraordinary saint I am. Rather, I tell it because I want to show how

11

different I am from God's Son, who came to Jacob's well seeking to make a true worshiper out of a Samaritan woman whom he met there.

With these two stories, you have two preachers and two women. But my episode with the woman on Broadway came and went in less than a minute. And I spent a good part of the next thirty minutes praying regretfully over that encounter, asking that despite all that I hadn't done or said, God would somehow reach this woman. I wished that I had said something about Jesus Christ, wished that I had asked her name and the name of the alleged child in need of diapers, wished that I had prayed with her and for her—wished, overall, that there had been more reality in the interchange.

On the other hand, Jesus said to the Samaritan woman in John 4:23, "A time is coming and has now come when the true worshipers will worship the Father in spirit and truth [that is, anywhere and genuinely], for they are the kind of worshipers the Father seeks." Our God seeks worshipers; he pursues them. I, on the other hand, barely began the process of helping this woman to become a genuine worshiper of our great God. That purpose wasn't even on my radar. I just reacted.

How different God is! He really goes after worshipers. In light of that kind of God, I want to consider three questions. First, how hard does God seek worshipers—or, put another way, how do we know that God really seeks worshipers? Secondly, why does God seek worshipers—out of an egocentric rushing after people to get them to worship him, praise him, honor him, and lift him up? That doesn't seem worthy of a God who tells us to be humble. Finally, my third question is: why should we say yes to God's search for us?

To begin, let us address the first question: how do we know that God seeks true worshipers, or how hard does God really seek them? The answer is that he seeks worshipers very hard. We know how hard he seeks them because he broke all the rules to engage the Samaritan woman. He was astonishingly proactive in searching out this woman. Think about it. First of all, he came down from heaven in search of people like this woman. The encounter between the Son of God and the woman at the well would never have happened if God had not determined long beforehand to put himself in a position where he could genuinely be thirsty. The incarnation underscores his search in a tremendous way. Jesus' plea in verse 7, "Give me a drink," was not an evangelistic gimmick employed by a disembodied voice to get into a religious conversation. Jesus, the Word made flesh, really was thirsty; that is why he asked the Samaritan woman for water. He had been walking all morning in the hot sun of Samaria, making his way from Judea in the south through Samaria, up to Galilee to the north. He was genuinely tired.

However, there was more to his search than coming to earth and showing up thirsty at Jacob's well. Jesus also threw aside all social caution and convention so that he could reach this particular woman who had so many strikes against her. First, Jesus spoke to a woman in public, something that a rabbi would never do, unless the woman was a relative. Secondly, he spoke to a Samaritan; a self-respecting Jew of that day would never have done that. Finally, he asked to share a drink with her, an outrageous expression of inappropriate intimacy in that culture. He did all this, knowing this woman's moral condition. She was terribly unclean, utterly unacceptable. Then, after his outrageous behavior got her attention, he went after her heart. He asked about her husband. He said, in effect, "Look, let's talk honestly about what's going on with you. Let's talk about your current relationship. Let's talk about why it is that you are here during the hottest part of the day, when no normal person would be here."

When Jesus proclaims that "God is spirit, and his worshipers must worship in spirit and in truth" (John 4:24), he isn't simply answering a question about the proper location for worship. He goes further, saying, "Look—please, lady, drop the religious subterfuge. Come clean; be real. God is looking for people who are worshiping in truth, so let's not just talk religion. Let's talk about what is really going on. You see, dear woman, God wants you. God wants *you*. God, the Sovereign One, seeks you, and he does not want some fake you. He is after the real you."

Every true worshiper has heard and responded to that voice. If you are really a worshiper in whom the Spirit of God has come to live, you have heard and continue to hear the voice of the incarnate God saying, "Come to me. I love you; I seek you; I want you. I want the real you. I love you that much."

That summons, of course, comes in a variety of forms. Let me give you two examples. During my seminary days, a fellow student nailed me with an intense and dead-on rebuke that left me reeling. God used him to tell me, "Charlie, get real." He used him to say, "Look, Charlie, where is the reality in your profession of faith, given what you have just done, given the way you have just behaved in that situation?" My wife has also been used by God many, many times down through the years to nail me about getting real. But you have to see that when someone nails you, it isn't just that person nailing you; the God who seeks your worship, who seeks the real you, is nailing you. If you just get mad at the messenger, you are missing what's going on. You are missing the God who seeks you.

Rebuke from others is not the only way God comes after you and me, not the only way he speaks to us. On other occasions, I have been swept off my feet by the God of grace. In these inexplicable moments, I have seen and felt such an immensity of undeserved and sometimes even unsolicited love, pouring out from him upon me, that I have had no adequate way to express my response. I remember once, when I was a teenager, shortly after one such experience, wanting desperately to run up and down the corridor in the dormitory of my boarding school, giving all my money away. (What restrained me was the realization that it was in fact my parents' money, and therefore I was not at liberty to give it all away.)

In both cases, whether brought about by a rebuke or by an overwhelming experience of the love of God poured out upon us, divine reality breaks in. God sought us; he found us; he made us worshipers. That is the astonishing thing about the God of the Bible, the God we worship. It is what sets him apart. It makes Christianity different from every other world religion. Our God pursues people. God seeks worshipers; we don't go after him. Unlike false religion, our faith is not something initiated by you or me at all. He finds us.

But so often we don't want the real thing. We don't want the real God breaking in, and so we use religion. We think we can use religion or antireligion—whatever works—to bargain with God or fate, so that we can get him or it to cooperate with our agenda. At other times, we use religion or antireligion to hide from God, to push him away. Anything but the real God will do. That is how we so often function.

We often treat God the way that we treat a traffic cop—slowing down when we think that one is in our area. When we think that God is watching, usually at church or in a crowd of religious people, we try to act in such a way that he won't "pull us over" and interfere with our plans to get wherever it is that we want to go. We just want to "keep our noses clean" religiously, so that God won't bother us. When we treat God like an interference to be avoided, we don't want God. We want religion when it looks good, but we don't truly want *him*. That's the tragedy of the human heart.

But God comes after us anyway. He doesn't give up. He pursues us very hard. In my religious tradition, when we baptize a baby, we see this pursuit with great vividness. The baby is totally clueless. At times, in fact, the baby strongly objects to being taken out of his parental comfort zone, put into the arms of a stranger who smells and feels different, and then sprinkled with water that is often too cold. But that's how it works. Even when we don't seek (or sometimes even want) God, he seeks us and claims us. He goes out of his way. He comes down from glory. He goes after losers like the Samaritan woman, like you, like me. He seeks us when we are running pell-mell away from him. He chases us and chases us, like the hound of heaven down the corridors of time, until he gets us—because he is that kind of God. That's how hard he seeks.

This leads us to our second question: why does God seek so hard for worshipers? Isn't it unseemly of God to seek people to love, praise, and worship him, to put him at the center of their existence? What would you think of me if I were to go to so much trouble to get you to worship me? What would you do if, Sunday after Sunday, your pastor stood up in the pulpit and told you not about Jesus, but about himself? If your pastor said, "I am the way," you might lock him up or at least fire him. For human beings, seeking praise and worship is unseemly, to say the least. So is it not unseemly of God to want his glory to be at the very center of the universe? Isn't he supposed to be humble?

Allow me to respond to this question. The unseemly thing about my own grandstanding would not be the grandstanding per se. The impropriety, the outright nonsense, would be to make such a demand in light of the reality of who I actually am. Every gift and opportunity that I have has been given to me graciously by God, the God who made me and has ordered my life providentially. I owe my very existence, at the moment when I am grandstanding, to the God who not only made me but, because he is the living water, literally sustains me at the very moment that I am showing off.

Let me say something here about what is called "natural law." Natural laws—say, the law of gravity or the laws governing the chemical bonds that hold together the molecules in our bodies and enable us to cry out loud, "Look at me! Am I not great?"—aren't really laws at all. At least, they are not laws in the sense that we usually mean: inevitable and impersonal processes. That definition fits with the view of deism, not of the Bible. What people call natural laws are in fact the expressions in real time of a faithful God's faithful and continuing activity. The eternal Son, by offering water to the Samaritan woman, offered to give her life. That cause and effect is how the world works, how God works. According to Hebrews 1:3, he upholds the universe by his word of power. Colossians 1:17 says that he actively holds everything together. Moment by moment, gravity continues to work. The reason you have not flown out of your chair is because right now, at this very moment, Jesus Christ is upholding what we call the law of gravity. We call it a law because it's predictable. It's predictable because Christ is faithful.

For me to speak and act as if I had life in myself, or as if my gifts and opportunities were my own doing, would be sheer idiocy. To suppose that people should rally around me, so that their lives might be integrated and empowered, would be sheer nonsense. It would not just be evil; it would be ridiculous. On the other hand, for God to tell everybody to rally around himself as the source of life, to seek our worship, to put himself at center stage, makes all the sense in the world, because he is truly worthy of all these things. God has chosen humility, but God has never chosen false modesty, because God is never false. When

Jesus offered water that would give eternal life, he wasn't falsely modest about what he could do.

The Grand Canyon deserves awe from us for the simple reason that it is awesome. To stand in awe of it is to respond truly or, to use Jesus' terminology in John 4:24, to respond "in truth." Likewise, to stand in awe of God is to respond according to truth. God, in other words, is worthy of our worship, and therefore it is anything but unseemly to worship him. It is anything but unseemly for him to ask us, to call us, to command us to worship him with all of our being, to love him with all our heart and soul and mind and strength.

Consider just two aspects of his worthiness: first, his immensity—the sheer size of his power and wisdom; second, his changing people without coercing them. First of all, God is immense. Jesus drives at this point in John 4:24 when he says that "God is spirit." What Jesus is getting at by calling God "spirit" is not that he is without physicality, but that he is uncontainable. The Samaritan woman had been discussing with him where the proper place to worship was supposed to be: Mount Gerizim or Mount Zion. His response was in keeping with Solomon's great prayer on the day when the great temple of old was dedicated: "The heavens, even the highest heavens, cannot contain you" (2 Chron. 6:18). By saying "God is spirit," Jesus was saying, "Woman, it's not this mountain or that mountain; not even the highest heavens can contain the God who calls you to worship him."

Think for a moment about the immensity of our God compared to the sun. The sun is at the center of our solar system, about 93 million miles away from the earth. Its light travels at 186,000 miles per second—seven and a half times around the circumference of the earth in one second. At that rate, the light of the sun takes eight and one-half minutes to get to us.

Because the sun's heat and light radiate spherically, all but an infinitesimally tiny portion of the sun's energy is simply wasted, as far as Earth is concerned. Yet that tiny proportion is enough to give us all the light and heat that we need—even more than we need sometimes. Now think about how this sun has been cranking out energy at that level, not just for a week, not just for a hundred years, but (as far as I can gather) for billions of years, self-consuming at an astonishing rate. Yet our sun is so huge that it hasn't come close to burning out. Such immensity of size and power and resource is staggering beyond meaningful calculation. We can do the numbers, but we can't take it in. And this sun is only one small, insignificant star among billions of stars in a universe that, as a whole, cannot hold God inside it. He is bigger and more powerful than the entire universe.

David is responding to the immensity of God in Psalm 8:

When I consider your heavens,
    the work of your fingers,
the moon and the stars,
    which you have set in place,
what is man that you are mindful of him,
    the son of man that you care for him? (vv. 3–4)

But David goes on to point out that God does think about us. We are on his mind; we are on his heart. God seeks relationship with us; he seeks worship from us; he is after us. In light of such a God, how unbelievably trivial it is that we should find ourselves arguing over which mountain is the right place to find him on earth—or, to modernize the question, about what color of carpet should be laid in the sanctuary or what style of music should be employed in public worship! Many churches divide over issues like that. How absurd!

A second glorious aspect of God that should fill us with wonder and praise is that he dramatically, powerfully, extraordinarily changes people—people like you and me —without coercing them. Think again about the story of the woman at the well. The uncontainable God came in human flesh to this woman and called her—the real her—to worship him. But he didn't blow her away with a demonstration of his terrifying power. Instead, he asked her for a drink, offered her a drink, called her to face her personal issues, and answered her religious questions. From the Bible's report of her telling all sorts of people about the man who had seen into her life, we know that this encounter changed her dramatically, but Jesus didn't force anything upon her.

The God we worship changes us far more profoundly than any tyrant could, yet he does so in a manner that doesn't usurp us. When the Romans captured the Gauls, they would sometimes put them in chains, drag them through a river, and tell them, "Okay, now you are Christians; you just got baptized." Tyrants and abusive parents bully us and for their efforts get, at best, reluctant, external compliance. But God doesn't work that way. How, then, does conversion happen? How does divine conquest, the absolute sovereignty of God in the salvation of a person, work? How does God's sovereignty in fulfilling his election from before the dawn of time coincide with human freedom? As a great Puritan prayer says, "To the eye of reason, everything respecting the conversion of others is as dark as midnight, but thou canst still accomplish great things. The cause is thine, and it is to thy glory that men should be saved."[1]

My own conversion and subsequent growth is a mystery to me. If you really think about yours, you will see that it is a great mystery as well. God changed my heart. By his sovereign choice,

---

1. *The Valley of Vision: A Collection of Puritan Prayers and Devotions*, ed. Arthur Bennett (1975; repr., Edinburgh, UK: Banner of Truth, 1986), 177.

he has done things in me and for me that I could not possibly do. God has changed my life profoundly, and he continues to do so, wooing me effectively from my many follies. Yet not once in my thirty years as a disciple of Jesus Christ have I ever felt coerced by him. Sometimes I have felt coerced by God's people, but I have never felt coerced by God. Yet he has conquered me far more dramatically than any human being ever could. He has won me over, and he still wins me over. I am, in fact, more fully myself with every victory he wins.

The Westminster Confession of Faith does nothing more than tell us what the Bible says about the wonderful mystery of the way in which God subdues us. The Confession reads in part: "God from all eternity, did, by the most wise and holy counsel of his own will, freely, and unchangeably ordain whatsoever comes to pass," including conversions, with his immense, unstoppable power, "yet so, as thereby . . .[is no] violence offered to the will of the creatures" (3.1). There is no sovereign like this sovereign. Every other sovereign in your life, even the sovereigns you have chosen, has imposed himself upon you and oppressed you. This sovereign sets you free. This sovereign makes you more fully yourself than you were before he conquered you. If you are a Christian, you know that what I am saying is absolutely true. If you are standing on the outside and are not a Christian, let me assure you that this is true. To give yourself up is not to lose yourself, but to find yourself. That is the mysterious way in which our God works, and it is why he is worthy of our praise.

This leads to my third and final question, which I have already really begun to answer: why should we say yes to this God who comes after us, seeks us, calls us to worship him, and sets about making us worshipers of himself? We should say yes to this God because it is the height of folly not to do so. Look at Jeremiah 2:12–13:

"Be appalled at this, O heavens,
    and shudder with great horror,"
            declares the LORD.
"My people have committed two sins:
They have forsaken me,
    the spring of living water,
and have dug their own cisterns,
    broken cisterns that cannot hold water."

In other words, they have traded a flowing stream for a leaking and stagnant hole in the ground. How absurd! How horrific! How dumb! Notice the twofold nature of this crime. Israel didn't just turn away from the God of living waters, the One from whom all life comes, the One from whom all goodness and all truth and all beauty flow. They also made up other gods to suit themselves, gods that proved to be worthless.

Israel's twofold crime points to something basic to every person—religious or not, atheistic or theistic. Everyone is wired to worship. We are always worshiping. We never stop. You are worshiping right now. You may be worshiping wrongly, but you are worshiping. We can't help it—God built us that way. We are always giving our hearts and our hopes to someone or to something—a leader or a relationship, a job or a future success. The question for you and me is: what or whom are you worshiping right now? Is that object of worship good enough and wise enough and strong enough to bear the weight of your life?

There is only one reality in the whole universe that is big enough and strong enough and consistent enough to bear the weight of your life. It is not happiness. It is not self-fulfillment. It is not a functional family. It's not success. It's not looking good at church or among peers or colleagues. It's not some version of America that you wish you could get back to somehow.

Don't make any of these things your god. They cannot bear the weight of that.

What is it that you can't bear the thought of losing? Let's be real about it. A child? A job? A reputation? Another question: what keeps you up at night worrying? Grades? The opinions of other people? Work projects? Finances? Some outcome that you cannot control? Yet another question: what is it that you are convinced you absolutely must have to be happy and fulfilled, but do not yet have? A marriage? A different marriage? A functional family again? A certain academic degree? Sex? Sex of a certain sort?

Now, these things are not necessarily all bad—but as I heard Dr. John Bettler say once, "They are very bad gods." If they drive your life right now, if you are losing sleep over them, if you are willing to turn everything upside down in order to get them, or if you are desperately afraid of losing them, that is proof positive that you have made them into gods. In that role, they are nothing but cracked cisterns that do not hold water. They have no life in themselves, and they will kill you.

Let me conclude with this thought: even though you are a sinner, you are much too glorious, too mysterious, too wonderful, and too complex a creature, made in God's image, to worship anything other than the true God. The God of staggering immensity lovingly stoops to conquer you without coercing you. If you shrink yourself down, denying yourself and your glory, you will kill yourself now and forever, trying to find life where it cannot be found. Find water at the hands of the God who made you. Find water at the hands of God incarnate, Jesus, the Son of God who knows you, who came in search of you so that you could worship him truly, who loved you so passionately that he died for you. Take water from him and give him the glory that he deserves, and you will live. There is no end to the life that comes from rivers of living water. It goes on and on and on, getting better and better. It carries you through death and brings you to glory. Drink from that water.

3

Sought by Christ to Worship

RICHARD D. PHILLIPS

AS WE APPROACH the topic "Sought by Christ to Worship," I want to begin with one of the most remarkable verses in the Bible, a verse pregnant with hope but also providing a little frustration: "There I will meet with you, and from above the mercy seat, from between the two cherubim that are on the ark of the testimony, I will speak with you" (Ex. 25:22). Usually when I talk about Exodus 25:22, I emphasize its good news, because it describes a place where the holy God will meet with sinners. He provides a place where we can come and exercise that for which we were made—the worship of God—and where we can also learn of him. "Mercy seat" is an appropriate name, because this meeting place is a provision of God's grace by his mercy.

Moses would come to the mercy seat when he went before the ark in the tent of meeting, when his face would glow. The mercy seat was where the propitiatory blood was poured. Once a year, the high priest would come into the presence of God, bearing the twelve stones symbolizing the twelve tribes of Israel. He brought the blood of a lamb, poured it on the mercy seat, and met with God.

That ritual, of course, is a picture of the Lord Jesus Christ in Old Testament garb. When talking about justification in Romans 3:25, Paul says that God provided Christ to be "a propitiation by his blood." "Propitiation" is from the same Greek word translated "mercy seat." God provided Christ to be the mercy seat, where God himself will meet with us so that we can worship him, and where he will speak all his will to us and reveal his glory to our hearts so that our hearts, like Moses' face, will shine with the glory of God. That fullness is why Exodus 25:22 is such a wonderful verse.

But in the time of Moses, there was frustration involving the mercy seat: it wasn't very easy to get to. It was revealed only to a small and remote nation. Unless you were an Israelite, you wouldn't even have known it existed. You wouldn't know that there was a place to meet with the true and holy God. Besides, unless you were Moses or a Levite or a member of the family of Aaron or the high priest, you would spend your whole life without ever seeing or coming to the mercy seat. So there was some good news and some bad news. The good news was that God had provided a place where sinners could meet with the holy God and could worship him, but the bad news was that you really could not get there.

I think that many people keenly feel the same problem today. They realize that God is holy and great. They have heard about nature's display of the glory and greatness of God, and they know that he is worthy to be praised. People see worship as a wondrous privilege. But, from where people stand, they just don't know how to get there. From where their lives are lived, they don't think that they will be able to meet with God. They hear what Jesus says in John 4:23 about the Father seeking worshipers, but it seems to them that it must be others whom the Father is seeking. Yes, there is a place where God will meet with mankind, even with sinners, but they can't see it or find it; they don't know how to get there. In short, for these people too, God's promise in Exodus 25:22 is not good news, but bad news.

In light of this problem of worship, the Reformed understanding of Scripture speaks profoundly. According to Arminianism, while Jesus has opened up a way to be saved and to worship God, you nonetheless must have what it takes to get there if you want to go through with it. I cannot tell you how many sermons I've heard make the point that Jesus has done his part, and now you must simply do yours. On the other hand, the Reformed faith, following the Holy Scriptures, tells us something more, something better. Jesus made a way—and then he came and got us. He came to seek us, and he himself by his sovereign, saving work brings us to God. We worship God, not because we have what it takes, but because Jesus has what it takes.

No place in Scripture shows this better than John 4. Although the chapter has many well-loved statements, perhaps the most glorious is verse 4: "And he had to pass through Samaria." Jesus had been in Judah and Jerusalem, where the Pharisees were hassling him, and now he wanted to leave that area and return to Galilee. But, geographically, Jesus did not have to pass through Samaria. Rather than travel straight north through Samaria, the Jews usually went around that territory, and there were many reasons for Jesus to go around it. But he "had" to go through Samaria because he had come to seek and to save the lost.

Dr. Barnhouse compared Jesus' situation to that of a soldier who has been overseas and arrives back in San Francisco. On his way home to Philadelphia, he "has" to go through Miami. Now that's not the most direct route. But if someone asked, "Why do you have to go through Miami?" he would reply, "My fiancée lives there." His route was determined by love. Similarly, Jesus had to go through Samaria because of his love for the lost and his determination to save them. In John 10:16, Jesus pictures himself as the Good Shepherd and says, "I have other sheep that are not of this fold. I must bring them also." That love is why Jesus had to go through Samaria.

For the same purpose, even today, Jesus has to go into the dark places where we are found, and the gospel has to be preached in every dark and dying corner of this world. If Jesus had come into this world only to open a way to God, he would never have needed to go to Samaria. What Jesus was going to do in Jerusalem would have been perfectly sufficient. Dying on the cross for our sins made a way. But Jesus had more to do than that. He brings us to God through our relationship with him. The Samaritans in John 4 would become worshipers of God in spirit and truth because they were personally sought by Jesus Christ and because, through their relationship with him, he broke down every barrier. Likewise, he removes every obstacle impeding our worship of God.

I want to look at four major barriers to worship, four reasons why we can't and won't worship, all of which are removed because Jesus is seeking us to worship God. Let's look at John 4. Verses 5–6a tell us that Jesus came to Jacob's well, near a town called Sychar in Samaria. Verses 6b–9 then read,

> Jesus, wearied as he was from his journey, was sitting beside the well. It was about the sixth hour.
> A woman from Samaria came to draw water. Jesus said to her, "Give me a drink." (For his disciples had gone away into

the city to buy food.) The Samaritan woman said to him, "How is it that you, a Jew, ask for a drink from me, a woman of Samaria?" (For Jews have no dealings with Samaritans.)

In these few verses, Jesus overthrew several barriers: cultural and ethnic, sexist, social and religious. First, he overthrew the cultural and ethnic barrier that separated the Jews from the Samaritans. In the eighth century BC, the Assyrians had conquered the northern kingdom of Israel. These Assyrians had a policy of deporting some people and replacing them with others. So the Ten Tribes were taken away, and other peoples from the region of Babylon were brought to live in the land. These new peoples believed in worshiping local gods, so they worshiped Yahweh, after a fashion. Because they did not worship Yahweh in the right way, he sent lions after them (2 Kings 17). But even though they sent a message to the Assyrian king, asking how they were supposed to worship the god of the area to which he had sent them, they also wanted to worship their old gods. So, through the centuries, this hybrid religion characterized the people of Samaria, who also gradually became a mixed breed among the Israelites. Notice that this Samaritan woman relates to "our father Jacob" (v. 12). However, the Jews hated the quasi-Judaism of the Samaritans so much that a rabbi from Jesus' era said that "he that eats the bread of the Samaritans is like one who eats the flesh of swine."[1] That harsh statement reflects a barrier of ethnic and cultural hatred reinforced by centuries of conflict. Yet Jesus simply crossed that barrier. There was no way that the woman could have crossed that barrier. If she had shown up in Jerusalem and said, "I am a Samaritan. I would like to worship the living God," they would have sent her away. But Jesus came to her.

1. See Jacob Neusner, *The Mishnah: A New Translation* (New Haven, CT: Yale University Press, 1991), 87.

Moreover, this Samaritan was a woman. It may not seem scandalous to us that Jesus was sitting at a well talking with a woman, but it most certainly was in Jesus' day, particularly among the Jews. Religious Jewish men did not speak even to their own wives in public. Any rabbi who did so would lose his reputation completely. Jewish men prayed daily, "Blessed art thou, O Lord, who hast not made me a woman." Yet Jesus unashamedly crossed that barrier, because he was seeking her.

The third barrier that he crossed involved social and religious taboos. Jews could not share utensils with Samaritans. If they did, they risked defilement, and what a headache it was to be rendered unclean. An unclean person couldn't go into the temple. Yet here Jesus deliberately crossed that line by asking the woman for a drink. You can see why she was astonished: "How is it that you, a Jew, ask for a drink from me, a woman of Samaria?" (v. 9).

How can we apply this to our day? Why don't people come to worship God? Here is the first reason: "I don't fit in. I just don't belong with those people, the ones in the place where God is to be worshiped." That may be the most common of all excuses today. Rich people think that Christianity is for the poor. Poor people think you have to have a fancy car to go to church. The educated say that the Bible is for simpletons, and uneducated people think that you have to be highly educated to go to church and listen to sermons. The strong say that Christianity is a crutch for the weak, and the weak say you can't go to church unless you have it all together. White people say that only black people can be spiritual, and black people say that Christianity is a white man's religion. No matter who you are, there is an instinct that says, "I just don't belong where God is worshiped."

And the truth is that we don't. This woman certainly did not. She did not belong in the religious world where God was

30

worshiped. She could not go to the place where the mercy seat was. The religion that produced Jesus Christ was alien to her, so he came to her. How was she to participate in the worship of God? Through her relationship with Jesus Christ.

You and I really don't belong in God's presence. We are part of the world below. But Jesus is seeking worshipers. So he crosses into our world, sits at the well where we are drawing our pail, and connects with us. He draws us to himself, brings us into his flock, and says, "This one has become my brother; this is my sheep." Hebrews 2:13 quotes Jesus saying, "Here am I, and the children God has given me" (NIV). If you belong with Jesus Christ, you belong with God.

I remember the circumstances that brought me to Jesus Christ. How unlikely they were! Though I was raised in a religious home, it was no closer to biblical faith than Samaritan religion was to Jewish biblical religion. We went to church, but we did not go to God. We were loving and moral people, but we had no sense of worshipping God and seeking his face, of glorifying him. I was not raised to need a savior; frankly, I was raised to be a savior. I was not raised to worship; I was raised to be worshiped. I would never on my own have ended up a Christian.

When it came to true worshipers, I just did not belong. I certainly did not belong in the church where I came to Jesus Christ. That church taught truth that I thought was ridiculous. I remember very well hearing certain doctrines that I now preach and thinking, "This man has lost his mind." The lifestyles that those believers led absolutely did not appeal to me. People talked about going to heaven, and I would say, "What would we be doing there? A better version of what we do in church? I don't want to do that." I just didn't belong before Jesus Christ came to me—before I came to him—and made me his own.

So how did a person like me become a Christian? Well, one answer might be "through circumstances." My military career had progressed to a certain point where I needed to get a different kind of job, and I got a letter from West Point asking if I wanted to teach there. But when I interviewed, the faculty department didn't really want me. But during a lunch break, I met the chairman of another department, and through that relationship, I eventually accepted a job at the University of Pennsylvania. As I moved into an apartment in downtown Philadelphia, a lady who lived next door was moving out. She was a young woman, and I was a gentleman, so I helped her carry some boxes to her car. In retrospect, I know she was a Christian. She was a witness to me. She said, "If you ever thought about going to church, you might try Tenth Presbyterian Church." That was her whole witness to me. My body language said, "Here I am carrying boxes to your car; did you have to bring that up?"

Several months later, God put an ache in my heart that I couldn't explain. Why wasn't I finding meaning or purpose or satisfaction in my life? Why did I end up saying, "What was that church again?" So I sat in a pew at Tenth Presbyterian Church with an aching in my heart, even though I could not understand why. Now I know why: because Jesus was crossing every barrier that I would never cross. He was seeking me, so that I would know God and worship him—just as Jesus is seeking you. All those reasons why you don't belong change when you see Jesus, hear his voice, and come to know him. Suddenly you will belong where he belongs, and that is where you will worship God.

Another barrier standing in the way of worship is one that people may scarcely be aware of, while also knowing it very well: we are not able. Our spiritual inability to seek after God, to worship him, to care about godly things, and to revel in him is indeed an obstacle. But it is one that Jesus comes to remove. As the woman in John 4 marveled that Jesus would sit and drink with her, Jesus said these amazing words: "If you knew the gift of God, and who it is that is saying to you, 'Give me a drink,' you would have asked him, and he would have given you living water" (v. 10). From the way that this woman responded, she clearly did not get it: "Sir, you have nothing to draw water with, and the well is deep. Where do you get that living water?" (v. 11). Now "living water" to her was what we call "running water." She had plumbing on her mind. She was thinking, "What a hotshot! He thinks he is better than Jacob. Jacob dug this great well; he thinks he can get running water." But look at Jesus' response: "Everyone who drinks of this water will be thirsty again, but whoever drinks of the water that I will give him will never be thirsty again. The water that I will give him will become in him a spring of water welling up to eternal life" (vv. 13–14).

What was Jesus talking about? Later, in John 7, Jesus speaks in a very similar way, and we are told that he is talking about the Spirit of God living within us, imparting eternal life and giving us a power that we lack. It's the life-imparting gift of the divine Spirit who enables us to worship God. Jesus uses the water from Jacob's well as a symbol and contrasts it with the spiritual blessing that the water he gives can provide. Even though a man may drink from a well like Jacob's—a very fine well, with some of the best water in the area—he will still thirst; he will still have deep and unfulfilled longings. That, of course, is one of the great messages that the Word of God brings into this world. Ours is a longing world. The men and women whom we know are thirsty. The best that this world has to offer is unable to assuage that thirst. Evangelist Arthur Pink once commented, "Whether he articulates it or not, the natural man the world over is crying, 'I thirst.' Why this consuming desire to acquire wealth? Why this craving for the honors and plaudits of the

33

world? Why this mad rush after pleasure, the turning from one form of it to another with persistent and unwearied diligence? Why this eager search for wisdom?"[2]

Today I am at Princeton Seminary. What a great institution of learning! Yet why is there thirst in the hallways? Why this endless searching for knowledge, this ransacking of the writings of the ancients, the ceaseless experimentation of our day? Why the insane craze for all that is novel? Because there is an aching void in the soul—something that remains unsatisfied in every natural man or woman. This is as true of the millionaire as it is of the pauper. Riches bring no contentment. It's as true of the globetrotter as is it of the rustic who has never been outside the bounds of his native county. Traveling from one end of the earth to the other and back again fails to discover the secret of peace. Arthur Pink also reminds us that "over all the cisterns of this world's providing is written in letters of ineffaceable truth, 'Whoever drinketh of this water *shall thirst again*.'"[3] Why? Because people were made by God, for God. Ours is a spiritual thirst. We are spiritual beings made to know and worship God, and so no natural resources can quench our thirst. What we need is to worship, yet we are unable to do so.

Jesus says that the gift he gives, his living water, will enable us to thirst no more. We will be able to worship. That offer is not just to the Samaritan woman. It's true for you; it's true for me. We may have all that the world can offer: riches, position, power. Yet, as businessman Lee Iacocca concludes, "Fame and power are for the birds"[4]—and this from a man who devoted

2. Arthur W. Pink, *The Seven Sayings of the Saviour on the Cross* (1984; repr., Grand Rapids: Baker, 2005), 103–4.

3. Ibid., 104, emphasis in original.

4. Lee Iacocca and Sonny Kleinfield, *Talking Straight* (New York: Bantam, 1988), 35.

his whole life to those things. How many times have we read the biographies of people who pursued glory or fame or pleasure, only to say at the end, "It didn't get me what I was thirsting for"?

But Jesus says, "Whoever drinks the water that I will give him will never thirst." That is a serious claim. It has to be backed up. But two thousand years of Christian experience does back it up. Whoever comes to him and drinks of him will never thirst. Jesus said, "I came that they may have life and have it abundantly" (John 10:10). That is what Jesus offers, and that is what we offer today in his name: not a list of rules, not a political agenda, not a superficial social association, but life welling up, springing forth unto eternal life, so that we will be able to worship God. Yet we wind up concluding, "But I just can't be that kind of person."

I remember very well a part of my journey when I badly wanted to be devout. I was drawn by the rudiments of religion— beautiful chapels, candles flickering in the dark. I wanted to develop mystical feelings. But I just couldn't do it. I couldn't relate to God. But Jesus says he will give us what it takes. As Isaiah 12:3 says, "With joy you will draw water from the wells of salvation." Psalm 36:8–9 also says, "They feast on the abundance of your house, and you give them drink from the river of your delights. For with you is the fountain of life." My favorite hymn written by Dr. James Boice speaks from this text:

Come to the waters, whoever is thirsty;
Drink from the Fountain that never runs dry.
Jesus, the Living One, offers you mercy,
Life more abundant in boundless supply.[5]

5. "Come to the Waters," in James Montgomery Boice and Paul Steven Jones, *Hymns for a Modern Reformation* (Philadelphia: Tenth Presbyterian Church, 2000), 21.

Like us, the Samaritan woman still didn't understand Jesus. We know that from her response in verse 15: "Sir, give me this water, so that I will not be thirsty or have to come here to draw water." She could not think beyond her material needs. That was her paradigm for life; it was all plumbing to her—nothing of the Spirit, no living stream. So Jesus pressed his pursuit of her more deeply. In verses 16–18, he changes his subject but not his goal. He goes after her, saying, "'Go, call your husband, and come here.' The woman answered him, 'I have no husband.' Jesus said to her, 'You are right in saying, "I have no husband"; for you have had five husbands, and the one you now have is not your husband.'"

In this section, several things are going on at once. First, Jesus is starting to reveal himself. He wants the woman to understand something: that he has divine knowledge. He knows things about her that he really couldn't know. At the same time, he is pressing upon her the truth about herself that she wants to avoid. The truth about this woman is that she has a sin problem. She has gone from man to man, and her present man is not her husband. No doubt this has been affecting her life. She is at the well at the sixth hour of day, about noon. People who have been at Jacob's well know that it is actually quite a hike from the village, and an ordinary woman would not make such a long trip to get water in the heat of the day. The truth probably was that she wasn't welcome in feminine society, and so sin was making a mess of her life. More importantly, sin was keeping her from God. That's what sin does.

Imagine the media hubbub if it were suddenly revealed that the best friend of a presidential candidate was a criminal. That news might have an effect on the polls. But God holds a higher office, and his reputation is more important than that of any presidential candidate. God cannot be God, he cannot be glorious, while associating with sinners like you, like me, like this woman. Her sin was not merely ruining her life; it was keeping her from God.

This reality brings us to the third barrier to our worship of God. The first reason was, "I just don't belong." This obstacle falls apart when Jesus crosses the barriers, joins you to himself, and declares that you belong to him. Then you say, "I just can't." But Jesus says that, if you will ask, he will give you spiritual life and power. Now the final obstacle is, "I am not worthy." The reason Jesus presses this upon the Samaritan woman is that he came to be the remedy for that problem.

Jesus accomplishes this as our mercy seat. Our sin keeps God from us and us from God, but Jesus' blood cleanses us. As John Donne put it,

> Wash thee in Christ's blood, which hath this might,
> That being red, it dyes red souls to white.[6]

That's what Jesus wanted for the Samaritan woman, and it is what Jesus wants for us.

I know how you feel. I also am just not worthy. But Jesus Christ came into this world to die for our sins and then to take his worthiness, the clean robe of his own perfect righteousness, and place it around your shoulders and say, "Now, come with me to God." The Old Testament is filled with pictures of this cloaking. One of my favorite images is Esther going before the king. What does she do before she gets there? She puts on her royal robe. You say, "Where might I get one of those?" Jesus says, "Here, take mine. I died for you. I fulfilled the law for you."

Author J. I. Packer puts it this way:

> Jesus Christ, by virtue of his death on the cross as our substi-
> tute and sinbearer, "is the propitiation for our sins" (1 Jn 2:2

---

6. John Donne, "Holy Sonnet IV," quoted in *The Poems of John Donne*, vol. 1, ed. E. K. Chambers (London: Lawrence & Bullen, 1896), 159.

KJV). Between us sinners and the thunderclouds of divine wrath stands the cross of the Lord Jesus. If we are Christ's, through faith, then we are justified through his cross, and the wrath will never touch us, neither here nor hereafter. Jesus "delivers us from the wrath to come" (1 Thess 1:10 RSV).[7]

And, let me add, he fits us to worship God.

When the woman realized that this was true, that Jesus was something special, she said, "Sir, I perceive that you are a prophet" (v. 19). In saying this, she also had another agenda—she turned to the sort of theological end run that every pastor knows so well. Why did she do that? As Charles Drew put it in the previous chapter, the you that Jesus wants is "the real you"—not the pretend you, not the masterfully self-deceived you, not the public-face you. Jesus wants the real you, because he makes provision for all that you lack. He is all that you aren't. He wants to bring you to God so much that his shed blood will wash away your sin. A later verse of Dr. Boice's hymn says,

> Come to the Savior, the God of salvation.
> God has provided an end to sin's strife.
> Why will you suffer the Law's condemnation?
> Take the free gift of the water of life.[8]

So it's true that we are not worthy of God, and that is a good reason for us not to worship. Yet Jesus comes to you and seeks you for worship.

The Samaritan woman is not able to face all of this yet, so she turns to another safe topic of theological dispute: "Our fathers worshiped on this mountain, but you say that in Jerusalem is

---

7. J. I. Packer, *Knowing God* (Downers Grove, IL: InterVarsity Press, 1973), 156.
8. "Come to the Waters," in Boice and Jones, *Hymns for a Modern Reformation*.

the place where people ought to worship" (v. 20). Nearby was Mount Gerizim, where the Samaritan temple once stood. The Jews said that worshipers had to go to Jerusalem. So she asks Jesus to clarify. Jesus answers honestly that the Jews are right, that one has to worship in Jerusalem: "Salvation is from the Jews" (v. 22). But then he gets back to his point. Do you see how persistent he is? He says, "The hour is coming, and is now here, when the true worshipers will worship the Father in spirit and truth, for the Father is seeking such people to worship him. God is spirit, and those who worship him must worship in spirit and truth" (vv. 23–24).

The woman is not inclined to take this answer. Maybe they can wait for the Messiah to arrive and can ask him, she offers (v. 25). Imagine saying that to Jesus Christ! He replies, "I who speak to you am he" (v. 26). The truth is that Jesus is the Messiah. He is the one who solves all our problems for worship, the one who breaks down all our barriers. "The blood of Christ, who through the eternal Spirit offered himself unblemished to God," says Hebrews 9:14, will "cleanse our consciences from acts that lead to death, so that we may serve the living God!" (NIV). That is why Jesus died: so that you could worship God. We are not able to worship apart from Jesus.

Look at Jesus' statement again. A more accurate translation of his words would be, "It is I AM who speaks to you." "I AM" was the voice that Moses heard from the burning bush. And the Samaritan's religious background would have further reminded her of God saying to Moses, "I am going to make the mercy seat where you may meet with Jehovah." *Jehovah* means "I AM," and now Jesus is saying to her, "I AM." Here the woman discovers that Jesus is the mercy seat. Here the final barrier is broken.

Why are people not coming to worship God? They say, "I don't belong," or "I'm not able," or "I am just not worthy."

Here is the glorious gospel, and the world perishing in darkness says, "I never knew." That is why Jesus comes to you. That is why he causes his Word to be preached. That is why Jesus creates that unsettled feeling in your heart that makes you willing to speak with him. That is why he sits by your well, as it were—wherever you have been placing your pail, whatever source of life you have been seeking that will never save your soul. Jesus comes to you so that you won't have to say, "I never knew," and he takes away every excuse. He reveals himself and says to you, "I AM."

As we consider Jesus' conversation with the Samaritan woman, we realize that we ought to be more forthright in our evangelism about the gift that God has for the world. Jesus says to her, "If you only knew." What a statement! Yet the message that Jesus proclaims warrants such boldness. We are not just saved from our sin; we are saved to receive what Jesus offers. He says to this woman—an outcast, such a sinner that her own people won't even let her come to the well with them—"If you only knew . . . you would ask me, and I would give you living water" (v. 10 NLT). That bold offer stands good today. If Jesus Christ is seeking you, if he is sitting by that well where you are found, he is still saying, "If you only knew." And if you do know, you need only ask of him. All barriers have been removed.

"Jesus, the problem is that I don't belong."

Jesus says, "Simply ask of me, and you will belong to me, and I will bring you to your God."

"Oh, Jesus, I am just not able to do it. I am just not that kind of person."

Jesus replies, "Simply ask of me, and I will fill you with the Spirit of the living God, like living streams flowing with eternal life."

"Jesus, I am just not worthy."

Jesus answers, "If you only ask of me, my blood will wash away your sin, and my own righteousness will be credited to your account before God."

"Jesus, if I only knew."

Jesus says, "I AM, and in myself I make the place where you may worship God."

Jesus is the answer to our every need. He is the solution to every reason not to worship God. He breaks down every barrier between us and the presence of God. He did this for the Samaritan woman, and what happened then? She ran back to the town and said, "Can this be the Christ?" (v. 29), and she led others to Jesus. In fact, they came crying with joy: "We know that this is indeed the Savior of the world" (v. 42).

John includes one final, wonderful detail in this account. In verse 28, he says that "the woman left her water jar." If you see in Jesus Christ the one who makes you belong in the company of your Creator, who enables you to do that for which you are made, and who will make you worthy in him to come to God, you won't need that water jar anymore. You will let it go, no longer seeking success, money, fame, and pleasure—all the little idols of the world. Eternally satisfied, the woman left behind her water jar to tell others about Jesus Christ.

Because Jesus sought this woman, she was able to experience life. Jesus' statements come together: "The Father is seeking worshipers," and "If you ask me, I will give you streams of living water welling up to eternal life." We were made to worship God, and that is life indeed. As we read in Psalm 16:11, "In your presence there is fullness of joy; at your right hand are pleasures forevermore." When you experience that joy, you will let go of your water jar and commit yourself to Jesus Christ.

We were made for glory, and that is why the wells of this world can never satisfy our souls. We were made for God, and that is why God's Son came seeking us to worship God in spirit and truth—that we might have life and have it abundantly, that an eternal spring might well up in us, the Holy Spirit of the living God, and that we would be able to worship.

The Bible ends with another invitation from the mouth of Jesus Christ, now glorified and exalted as Lord: "Whoever is thirsty, let him come; and whoever wishes, let him take the free gift of the water of life" (Rev. 22:17 NIV). Don't say, "I don't belong." Don't say, "I can't." Don't say, "I don't deserve it." Don't say, "I never knew." Come to Jesus Christ and be found in him. Come and drink. Worship and live.

4

Guided by God's Sovereign Providence

JOSEPH "SKIP" RYAN

A FEW YEARS AGO, my wife and I were arriving back at Dallas/Fort Worth International Airport. DFW is a hub for one of the major airlines in our country. Hub airports were a good idea when they were created in the 1970s, but there are some problems with them now, and we experienced one of those problems when we landed that day. We had been visiting our son in California, and we had planned to arrive in Dallas just in time for an important event honoring a dear friend of ours. As we landed, I noticed that the pilot had to do some deft maneuvering to come through the storm clouds. As he brought the plane to a stop on the runway, he announced, "Ladies and gentleman, I have some good news and some bad news. The good news is that we are on time. The bad news is that, because of the storms, no planes have left DFW in the last two hours, and we do not have a gate available." I looked at my wife Barbara and said, "Two hours." She looked at me said, "Skip, heaven rules."

Now, my mind immediately began composing a letter to the president of American Airlines to tell him exactly how he could solve the problems of a hub where he had too many airplanes on the ground and not enough gates, and how he could file planes in and out of the gates so that at least the passengers who had landed and wanted to get off the airplanes could do so. As I started talking to Barbara about my idea, she said, "Skip, heaven rules."

About forty-five minutes later, the pilot came on and said that we might have noticed that it was getting a little warm. Unfortunately, the air conditioner was not working. He explained that they were hoping to have a generator brought to the plane in a half hour or so, and he apologized for the inconvenience. Barbara looked at me and said, "Skip, heaven rules."

Now, the issue for me that day was a very practical one. It wasn't simply that we missed entirely the event we had been looking forward to; it was that I didn't like to be out of control. I actually had two hours before getting off the plane to think it over, and the two hours were shaped by the preposterously short sermon my wife had given me. What I realized was this: when I think I am in control, I am really being presumptuous, and when I am out of control and believe that I ought to be in control, I am being presumptuous again.

"Heaven rules" is really a way of expressing the deep, wonderful truth of Scripture that we call *providence*. *Providence* in English combines the two Latin roots "pro" and "video": "pro" means "before," and "video" means "to see." Literally, the word means "to see beforehand." The great preacher Charles Spurgeon said, "Fate is blind; providence has eyes."[1] In modern usage,

1. C. H. Spurgeon, in *Spurgeon's Sermons*, vol. 5 (New York: Robert Carter & Brothers, 1883), 378.

providence is the great biblical teaching that everything that happens in the universe is accomplishing God's sovereign purposes. Now, the problem is that many of us don't like being out of control, and so we very quickly move from providence to presumption. We believe that God is in control until his being in charge moves us in a direction that we don't want to go. Then we question his wisdom, his goodness, his power, or the ability of American Airlines to get people off its airplanes. While God has certainly called us to be initiators and not to just live in the midst of wrong circumstances, how quickly our attempt to control things moves into the realm of presumption.

James, the author of the epistle, considers three kinds of presumptions and answers each thoughtfully through his great teaching on God's providential care in our lives. The first type is planning presumption, the second is personal presumption, and the third is positional presumption.

The first way that we move from providence to presumption is by forgetting how quickly our plans change. Look at James 4:13–14: "Come now, you who say, 'Today or tomorrow we will go into such and such a town and spend a year there and trade and make a profit'— yet you do not know what tomorrow will bring." James is talking about someone who is planning his yearly calendar, something that we all do. We look ahead, which as stewards we should indeed do, and yet we must do so with the frame of mind that we really don't know what the next day holds. We really cannot claim to see ahead. Despite our great technology, we do not have a "pro video" to allow us to see what is going to happen tomorrow.

So often our plans are made, we begin to execute them, and we become frustrated with any change that challenges our planning presumption. How quickly life changes. You get that phone call that you didn't expect from the doctor's office, or your boss comes in with news that will affect your future, or you travel to attend a conference and meet someone who is going to change the direction of your whole life. Planning presumption is rationally preposterous when you see how quickly things change.

The second way that we move from providence to presumption is by forgetting how quickly we change. Let's call that personal presumption. This presumption is what James addresses when he asks, "What is your life? For you are a mist that appears for a little time and then vanishes" (4:14). Under planning presumption, we forget that the content of tomorrow is unknown. Now what James is saying is that the very existence of our tomorrow is unknown. Recent world events have made that painfully clear. How much our world has changed! Terrorism and natural disasters alone have dramatically changed billions of lives in unexpected ways. We are constantly reminded that our own existence is much more fragile than perhaps we thought. In fact, James lists three things very quickly in a row to describe our lives. We are insubstantial (a mist), we are transient (here for just a little time), and we are gone without a trace (we vanish). If this perspective sounds a little pessimistic, let me suggest that it's realistic.

This realism means that we are dependent upon God, not self-sufficient. Yet we move from providence to presumption by forgetting that our position in relation to God never changes. I call this positional presumption. We forget our dependence upon God. James 4:15 says, "Instead you ought to say, 'If the Lord wills, we will live and do this or that.'" Sometimes you will hear Christians say, "Lord willing, I am going to New York tomorrow." Years ago, people used to punctuate their letters with the letters d.v., *divinitas volunteras*, Latin for "if God wills." Sometimes this convention may sound like pious chatter to us. In fact, John Calvin points out, "We read everywhere in the Scriptures that the holy servants of God spoke unconditionally of future things." He observes that, instead of focusing on *saying* "Lord willing," they were more concerned with *believing* it. "They had it as a principle fixed in their minds, that they could do nothing without the permission of God,"[2] and, because that idea was so firmly fixed in their minds and in the way that they lived, they did not need to say the words that much.

People who live by the fixed principle of God's providence do not forget how quickly life changes. They do not forget how quickly they change, and they do not forget that their dependence upon God never changes. Now, it is a hard thing to admit our dependence, but the issue is not a matter of admitting where our weakness is; it's really a recognition of where our strength lies. Upon what do you want to rest your tomorrows: your ability to make certain things happen, or the power of an infinitely strong and infinitely good God? Where do you want your security to lie? When we take the reins of life into our own hands, we forget that we do not have a "pro video" camera. We forget that we just don't know what will happen. We forget that we are mist. We forget, most of all, our dependence. So we plan our day or week or year. To quote a commentator on the book of James, Alec Motyer, we live "as if we were lords of earth and time."[3]

When we are presumptuous like this, we really become practical atheists. Regardless of what we say we believe about our God, in practice we are saying that we really believe in ourselves—our ability to control events, our ability to make things happen. None of this discredits our stewardship over our lives, which God has outlined in his Word, but how often we forget our realistic place in God's time!

2. John Calvin, *Commentaries on the Catholic Epistles*, trans. and ed. John Owen (Edinburgh: Calvin Translation Society, 1855), 340.
3. J. A. Motyer, *The Message of James* (Downer's Grove, IL: InterVarsity Press, 1985), 161.

Motyer also says, "[The years] go in a straight line from eternity to eternity, and on that line we receive another day neither by natural necessity, nor by mechanical law, nor by right, nor by courtesy of nature, but only by the covenanted mercies of God."[4] Many of us don't have any trouble talking about God's absolute control of the universe at the beginning of time, and many of us don't have much trouble speaking about God's absolute control of the universe as we move to the end of time, whatever that is going to look like. It's everything in between that we doubt. In practical ways, we live as if it all depends upon us.

What I am really talking about here is that great teaching of the Bible called providential concurrence. It means that God directs everything that happens, but does so in a way that does not violate natural or human participation. In other words, man has dominion, has stewardship over creation, has responsibilities to be exercised, but God nevertheless works out his plan through all of those human actions.

We see many things as natural occurrences, but we forget what lies behind them. For example, a meteorologist rightly defines a thunderstorm in terms of wind currents and energy changes, but Psalm 135:7 says, "He it is who makes the clouds rise at the end of the earth, who makes lightnings for the rain and brings forth the wind from his storehouses." Which is true? Both are. A botanist can tell us how vegetation grows, and she is right, but it is also true to say with Psalm 104:14, "You cause the grass to grow for the livestock and plants for man to cultivate, that he may bring forth food from the earth." A physicist may explain, given the right amount of information about the size, weight, and direction of a pair of dice, why they roll and land as they do, but it is also true to say with Proverbs 16:33, "The

4. Ibid., 162.

lot is cast into the lap, but its every decision is from the LORD." The Bible's teaching about what we call *providential concurrence* is that God directs and works through the distinctive properties of each created thing, so that these things themselves bring about the results that we see. So we can say that events are 100 percent caused by God, the Creator, and we can also say that, from our vantage point, they are 100 percent caused by the sequence of human events, invention, and activities that we observe and in which we participate.

The line between practical atheism and trusting in God's providential care is a thin one, and it's determined by your answer to this question: is God the primary cause that plans and initiates everything? Creaturely causes are vital, but they are rightly understood as concurrent or secondary causes, even though they may be the cause most evident to us. What is true in seemingly random events like grass growing and dice being thrown is really true of all human activity. Psalm 139:16 says that God our Father plans "every one of . . . the days that were formed for me, when as yet there was none of them." All our actions are under his providential ordering, "for 'In him we live and move and have our being'" (Acts 17:28). "It is not in man who walks to direct his steps," according to Jeremiah 10:23. Success and failure come from God: "Not from the east or from the west and not from the wilderness comes lifting up, but it is God who executes judgment, putting down one and lifting up another" (Ps. 75:6–7). According to 1 Corinthians 4:7, talent and ability come from the Lord: "What do you have that you did not receive? If then you received it, why do you boast?"

How profoundly insightful are these writers of Scripture! They know the way we work; they know the way we think; they know that we keep trying to take back those two hours on the tarmac at DFW and that we keep forgetting my wife's little sermon in all of our lives and in all of our actions, whether it's dealing with hurricanes or dice or delays. God's actions are the primary causes of outcomes, but in such a way that he makes room for, and indeed even elevates, our choices to a high level of responsibility and importance. Our actions are always significant, and from our point of view they seem determinative. But God's providence is primary. So all of our days, all of our successes and failures, all of our abilities and inabilities, all of our joys and disappointments, come from the hand of God, even as we act out our parts.

Spurgeon also says, "Fate and chance are blind, but Providence has eyes." While I would never presume to change Spurgeon's idea, I think something needs to be added to it. Providence not only has eyes, but it has heart. The word *providential*, in the way Christians use it, is almost always accompanied by a second word: *care*. God has providential care over us and over everything. God moves on his people's behalf. God bends all of history and all circumstances for our ultimate benefit. This is true in the seemingly small things, like waiting two hours on the runway at DFW, as well as in the big things. My daughter Kerry, at age sixteen, having just gotten her license, found herself driving down a highway with a drunk driver headed straight toward her, in her lane. At the last minute, with a flick of her wrist, she moved her car out of harm's way, and she and her friend walked away unhurt from a car that was slammed into a guardrail and totaled. That's providential care.

But remember that God's providential care was evident in the bending of all history for his purposes when he did not spare his own Son from a head-on collision. God's providential care worked out his purposes even in the most evil thing that men ever did: "This Jesus, delivered up according to the definite plan and foreknowledge of God, you crucified and killed by the hands of lawless men" (Acts 2:23). Do you see it? God delivered him up, but men acted concurrently—and, in this case, very poorly. Jonathan Edwards describes providence this way: "God not only does his people good; he *is* his people's good." God is our good in the gospel of his Son. He turned the wickedness of men on its ear by making the death of his Son the fullest expression of his providential care for us, and he did it concurrently with the desires and actions of men. You may have heard this before: "Who killed Christ? Judas, for money; Pilate, for power; the Pharisees, for envy; but the Father, for love."

I have a twenty-two-year-old son. Not long ago, he was a little boy playing in a bathtub. Now he's a senior at Stanford, loving football and enjoying acting. This young man is my joy, and I frankly cannot imagine giving him up. I cannot imagine giving my son over to the presumption of wicked people or wicked hands. The Father's love—the Father of Christ, but also the Father of us—is beyond me.

In our planning presumption, we forget how quickly our plans change; in our personal presumption, we forget how quickly our lives change; and in our positional presumption, we forget that our dependence upon God never changes. Presumption grabs the reins of our calendars, our lives, our tomorrows. James says that presumption boasts in arrogance and pride, pointing out how quickly we boast in futile things—for example, in our wealth:

> Come now, you rich, weep and howl for the miseries that are coming upon you. Your riches have rotted and your garments are moth-eaten. Your gold and silver have corroded. (5:1–3)

What strong words! But James puts them in the context of presumption. Now, I don't know how rich you are, and I don't know how much you presume upon your wealth. I don't know how much you presume that your education will guarantee you a secure future. But I do know the danger that lurks in every heart of moving quickly from trusting in God's providence to depending on our own ability to control things.

Whatever you may think of his military choices, Robert E. Lee was a great man who said, "The truth is this: The march of Providence is so slow, and our desires so impatient; the work of progress is so immense and our means of aiding it so feeble; the life of humanity is so long, that of the individual so brief, that we often see only the ebb of the advancing wave and are thus discouraged. It is history that teaches us to hope."[5] He was really saying what Søren Kierkegaard said in another way: "Life can only be lived forwards, but it can only be understood backwards."[6] Again and again we presume that we will understand our lives going forward. But Lee was right. Our presumption is humbled when we see how little we are, how little we have been in control, how little we can affect our tomorrows, how quickly we can lose what is valuable to us, and how our abilities will fail and fall in the tide of time.

But I would respectfully change one word of Lee's statement. It is not so much history that teaches us hope. It is the cross of Christ. The cross humbles our presumption. If God purposed for his Son to die for all of our sin, including our many sins of presumption, and if God bent all of history and the hearts of wicked men to accomplish the death of his benevolent Son for

5. Letter from Robert E. Lee to Lieutenant Colonel Charles Marshall, September 1870.
6. This is a commonly quoted variant of Kierkegaard's original wording, "It is quite true what philosophy says: that life must be understood backwards. But then one forgets the other principle: that it must be lived forwards," from his *Journals*, section IV A 164 (1843), quoted in Søren Kierkegaard, *Papers and Journals: A Selection*, trans. Alastair Hannay (New York: London, 1996), 161.

us, then can we not trust his providence to order our life and our tomorrows, just as he ordered our yesterdays? The argument is from the greater to the lesser. Paul makes that argument in Romans 8:32: "He who did not spare his own Son but gave him up for us all, how will he not also with him graciously give us all things?" If God has already given to us the greatest gift, his Son, will he fail for one second to order our lives for our good?

Robert E. Lee had a simple suggestion for how he, along with anyone else, could face even the most terrible trials and disappointments and could even pray for his enemies in the midst of those trials. He believed that people should do their best, according to the light that they have been given at the time, and should recognize that what they want might not be what God intends. In the last five years of his life, when he was beginning what became known as Washington and Lee University, he used to jot down on his desk little notes as thoughts came to him. After his death, a stack of these maxims was discovered in a drawer, and the shortest of them read like this: "God disposes. This ought to satisfy us."[7] That is, in short, the great biblical teaching of God's providential care. God disposes, and that should make our hearts glad.

7. Quoted in A. L. Long, *Memoirs of Robert E. Lee* (London: Sampson Low, Marston, Searle, and Rivington, 1886), 485.

5

Redeemed by God's Sovereign Mercy

PHILIP GRAHAM RYKEN

HOW REFRESHING it is to praise God together for his sovereignty! John Piper spoke in Minneapolis at a conference on the theme of God's sovereignty, particularly as it relates to suffering. Piper began that conference with these words: "The approach that I'm going to take tonight is not to try to solve the problem . . . of the sovereignty of God, but to celebrate it."[1] In a way, that's my purpose as well—particularly to celebrate God's sovereignty in salvation.

Whenever we talk about the sovereignty of God, we immediately run into one intellectual difficulty or another, as well as some practical difficulties. No aspect of the sovereignty of God is easy for us to understand. For example, God's sovereignty over

---

1. John Piper, "Ten Aspects of God's Sovereignty over Suffering and Satan's Hand in It" (address presented at the Desiring God 2005 National Conference, Minneapolis, MN, October 7, 2005).

creation is so hard for people to accept that a secular, materialist culture has come up with its own alternative creation story. On the other hand, I think of God's sovereignty over suffering and evil—again, a very difficult problem. One well-known evangelical theologian, wrestling with the aftermath of Hurricane Katrina, concluded that he could accept the terrible things that had happened only if God were not fully in control of these things. In other words, he concluded that the only way to deal with the problem is to say that God is not really God.

Now, the sovereignty of God over creation and over suffering are both hard concepts, but I doubt whether any is more difficult than God's sovereignty in salvation. Are we entirely saved by the work of God, or do we play some role in achieving our salvation—at least in choosing God? If God is fully sovereign in salvation, then isn't he somehow to blame for those who reject him and are damned? Those are hard questions, and I am not sure I can give fully satisfactory answers, but I can at least tell you what the Bible says about the sovereignty of God's mercy in redemption, and maybe we can celebrate that together in a way that will help us to give glory to God.

I want to focus mainly on Romans 9, but before we turn our attention there I want to set the stage by reminding you of two men who are mentioned in that chapter. These men were on different sides of the mercy of God: one man rescued by the sovereign Lord and one destroyed by him, one man saved and the other lost. I am speaking of Moses and Pharaoh. Let me remind you of a few things about the experience of these men.

Moses had a glorious experience on top of God's mountain (see Ex. 33). He had a vision of divine glory, and he rejoiced in the revelation he was given. He had prayed that he would be able to see something of the glory of God. That episode itself is surprising, because in his first encounter with God, he really did not want to see God's glory. When God appeared to Moses at the burning bush, Moses hid his face from the glory of God (Ex. 3). It wasn't just that he did not want to see the glory of God; he did not want to live with the glory of God, either. When God gave him an opportunity to serve him by leading his people into their deliverance, Moses said, "Oh, my Lord, please send someone else" (Ex. 4:13). How things changed during Moses' life! A man who couldn't bear to see the glory of God and who didn't want to pursue God's purpose for him became one who, more than anything else, wanted the glory of God to be demonstrated in his life. Obviously, something significant happened in the life of Moses to bring about that kind of spiritual change.

What a contrast there was between Moses and Pharaoh, a man who never learned to live for the glory of God! One of them made it to the mountaintop; the other was lost at sea. What was the difference between them? Why was it that Moses was saved and Pharaoh was lost? Well, if you didn't know the background of these two men, you might think it had something to do with their education and a difference in the way that they were trained. Surely in America we know the value of education and the difference it makes in someone's life. But Moses was raised at Pharaoh's court. In fact, the Scripture says that Moses was educated in all the wisdom of the Egyptians. So the difference between these two men had nothing to do with where they "went to college."

Then maybe the difference had something to do with their ethics. Maybe Moses was just a better person. Surely the things mentioned in Scripture about Pharaoh are not very flattering; he was a genocidal tyrant. But when you look closely at Moses' actions, you see that at heart he was no different. Remember when he decided to deliver Israel from Egypt by killing one Egyptian at a time? Really, that was the same approach that

Pharaoh was taking. Moses just had more limited means to give vent to the evil that was in his heart. Both of them in their hearts were equally guilty.

Maybe what made Moses different was his ethnicity. He was a Hebrew, of course, but that ethnic origin does not explain why Moses sought the glory of God. There were many other Hebrews, but only Moses was given this vision.

I suppose most people would say that, in the end, it comes down to free will, to the choice that these two men made in response to God—and certainly, in a way, that's true. Moses did make a decision to follow God. Hebrews 11 says that when Moses had grown up, he chose to be mistreated along with the people of God, rather than enjoy the pleasures of sin. Of course, Pharaoh made the opposite choice. He was given every opportunity to glorify God by letting God's people go; yet again and again he rejected that opportunity. He refused to listen. He hardened his heart, making a deliberate decision to set himself against the sovereign God.

Yet not even free will fully explains the difference between these two men. Even before Pharaoh hardened his heart, in a sense, the sovereign God hardened it for him. That's what the Scripture says. God announced this in advance, as he foresaw his providential working in the life of Pharaoh. God said, "I will harden his heart, so that he will not let the people go" (Ex. 4:21). On the other hand, does free will really explain the choice that Moses made? Remember that, given the choice at the beginning, he didn't want to follow God. He needed God to intervene in his life and to give him a desire to lead the people of God.

So what was the difference between these two men? It was the mercy of God, the sovereign intervention of divine mercy. It was the mercy of the God who had said to Moses, when he was up on that mountaintop, "I will have mercy on whom I will have mercy, and I will have compassion on whom I will have compassion" (Ex. 33:19 NIV). By the sovereign will of God, Moses was ordained for mercy—and, if you reflect for even a few moments on the whole life of Moses, you will see that it was just one mercy after another. The mercy of God delivered him from drowning when his mother had to, in effect, put her heart in the basket and set Moses out on the river, where he surely would perish. By the mercy of God, he was rescued by Pharaoh's daughter. The mercy of God prepared Moses for many years to lead the people of God. All the years that he spent in Pharaoh's court and all the things that he learned there prepared him for his future service. It was the mercy of God that called him into ministry. The mercy of God led him out into the wilderness for further preparation. Most especially, it was the mercy of God that forgave Moses all his sins. Moses was the one who taught the people of Israel that they should offer a lamb that first Passover, that they should spread the blood on the doorposts. He was the one who first understood what atonement and forgiveness and mercy meant. He lived his whole life under the mercy of God.

If you are a believer in Jesus Christ, that's your testimony. It's been mercy after mercy: mercy that God brought you to life, mercy even in your suffering, mercy in what you have experienced because God has been working his purpose out in your life. When someone asks what has made the difference in your life, you don't mention your education or ethnic background or family situation. You say it was the mercy that God had on you, specifically the mercy that God had on you in Christ.

As believers, we give the same testimony that the apostle Paul gave when he said, "When the kindness and love of God our Savior appeared, he saved us, not because of righteous things we had done, but because of his mercy . . . poured out on us generously through Jesus Christ our Savior" (Titus 3:4–6 NIV). Moses is the perfect example of the mercy of God. His story reminds us of the mercy that God has had on us, while Pharaoh is perhaps the perfect example of how, although God has mercy on whom he wants to have mercy, he also hardens those whom he wants to harden. God passed Pharaoh by; he left him in his sins. And as we compare these two men, we are being shown the mystery of the sovereignty of God in salvation.

In the mystery of election, the mystery of mercy, these two men are showing us a fundamental principle of God's dealings with humanity: God's grace is God's choice. We know that Moses and Pharaoh teach us this principle, because that is what the Scripture says in Romans 9. Now that we have the background of these two men, we are ready to see what Scripture says about God's sovereignty in salvation.

Before we read Romans 9:1–24, I want to present a basic outline. In the first five verses, Paul is agonizing over the problem of Israel. God had always promised salvation to the Jews, and yet many of them had rejected Jesus. They seemed to be cut off from grace. That problem raised the question whether perhaps God's promise had somehow failed. That question reminds us of some of our own questions about the people we love who have not yet come to Christ. The answer to this problem of Israel is that God never intended to save each and every person (vv. 6–13). He operates on the basis of election. There are always some who reject his salvation. Now that immediately raises a number of objections, and Paul considers them. In verses 14–18, he considers the objection that God's election is unfair. It is in this section that he refers specifically to Moses and Pharaoh. The second objection is raised in verse 19: if God's mercy is God's choice, there is nothing we can do about it. However, Paul answers that in the verses that follow:

I am speaking the truth in Christ—I am not lying; my conscience bears me witness in the Holy Spirit—that I have great sorrow and unceasing anguish in my heart. For I could wish that I myself were accursed and cut off from Christ for the sake of my brothers, my kinsmen according to the flesh. They are Israelites, and to them belong the adoption, the glory, the covenants, the giving of the law, the worship, and the promises. To them belong the patriarchs, and from their race, according to the flesh, is the Christ, who is God over all, blessed forever. Amen.

But it is not as though the word of God has failed. For not all who are descended from Israel belong to Israel, and not all are children of Abraham because they are his offspring, but "Through Isaac shall your offspring be named." This means that it is not the children of the flesh who are the children of God, but the children of the promise are counted as offspring. For this is what the promise said: "About this time next year I will return, and Sarah shall have a son." And not only so, but also when Rebekah had conceived children by one man, our forefather Isaac, though they were not yet born and had done nothing either good or bad—in order that God's purpose of election might continue, not because of works but because of him who calls—she was told, "The older will serve the younger." As it is written, "Jacob I loved, but Esau I hated."

What shall we say then? Is there injustice on God's part? By no means! For he says to Moses, "I will have mercy on whom I have mercy, and I will have compassion on whom I have compassion." So then it depends not on human will or exertion, but on God, who has mercy. For the Scripture says to Pharaoh, "For this very purpose I have raised you up, that I might show my power in you, and that my name might be proclaimed in all the earth." So then he has mercy on whomever he wills, and he hardens whomever he wills.

You will say to me then, "Why does he still find fault? For who can resist his will?" But who are you, O man, to answer back to God? Will what is molded say to its molder, "Why have you made me like this?" Has the potter no right over the clay, to make out of the same lump one vessel for honorable use and another for dishonorable use? What if God, desiring to show his wrath and to make known his power, has endured with much patience vessels of wrath prepared for destruction, in order to make known the riches of his glory for vessels of mercy, which he has prepared beforehand for glory—even us whom he has called, not from the Jews only but also from the Gentiles? (vv. 1–24)

What a difficult passage this is! The late James Montgomery Boice, a mentor to many in ministry, described this as the most difficult passage in the Bible—the hardest to understand, perhaps the hardest to teach. You will have noticed that it opens with an apostle in anguish. Paul is wrestling with the question that surely every believer has wrestled with: why are some people saved while others perish? Anyone who has received Christ wants everyone to receive the same free gift of eternal life, and yet not everyone becomes a Christian. Why not?

To Paul, this question was partly historical. He knew what the Scriptures had promised about the salvation of Israel, that the Jews were God's chosen people, and that they had received all the blessings that he mentions: adoption, the law, the covenant, the temple, all the promises of the Old Testament. They were even related to Jesus. Yet for all these privileges, many Jews of Paul's day had rejected the Messiah, refusing to receive Jesus as Savior and Lord.

How distressing that response was for Paul, because for him, it wasn't just a historical question. It was deeply personal. He had preached the gospel in synagogue after synagogue all over the Roman world, and yet many Jews were rejecting the gospel. Some were even trying to kill him. These were people he loved, his own flesh and blood, and so he speaks here of the great sorrow and unceasing anguish that he has for them. He is so upset that he is willing to die in Israel's place, much as Moses once offered to have his own name blotted out of the Book of Life if only the people of Israel would be saved.

Here we are given God's blessing to agonize over the fate of the lost. We are living at a time when many people deny that God would ever condemn anyone. Some people these days are trying to upgrade hell; others are trying to argue that everyone will be saved in the end or that there will be some way for us to rescue people from hell after death. That's obviously not what Paul believes. That's why he is in such anguish of soul. Significantly, it's not what Jesus believed either, as is clear from his teaching in the Gospels—in Luke 16, for instance. What urgency this gives us in our own proclamation of the gospel! What anguish it gives us when people do not come to Christ, because we understand from the Scriptures that those who die without Christ will be lost forever! And if we ourselves have not anguished over these lost ones and wrestled with their condition as Paul does, it is doubtful that we really understand what is at stake in the salvation of sinners or what the destiny of human souls will be.

As Paul wrestled with this, deeply troubled in his soul, he tried to reconcile what was happening with these people who were rejecting Christ with what he saw in Scripture, and he recognized that some people would reach the conclusion that somehow God's word had failed. If God had promised salvation to Israel, but Israelites were not saved, did that not disprove the truth of God's word? In verse 6, Paul flatly denies that conclusion. God's word has not failed. Then Paul explains why: because not all who are descended from Israel belong to Israel. He confronts a very common attitude in his day. Many Jews assumed that they were God's children simply because they were descended from Abraham. Paul is saying very clearly here that salvation has never been merely a matter of heredity. In effect, there had always been two Israels: the true Israel and the false Israel. As he says in Romans 2:28–29, a man is not a Jew if he is one only outwardly. No, a man is a Jew if he is one inwardly. There he is really talking about what it means to be a believer. It's a matter not of something outward but of something inward.

What a major theme this is all through the Old Testament! It's an issue that often comes up in the historical record of the people of God. Not every Israelite believed in the promise of God, and therefore not every Israelite was saved. Of course, we could say the same thing about contemporary Christianity. Not everyone who goes to church is a Christian. In the biblical sense of the word, being a Christian is a matter of believing in Jesus Christ, but not everyone does that—not even in evangelical churches, and not even in Reformed churches. So even in our present age, the distinction exists between the true church and what is merely the outward church. That was also true in Israel. If people rejected Christ, it was not then God's failure or the failure of his word, but their own failure for not receiving Christ by faith.

In verse 6, Paul states the general principle that not every Israelite is among the elect. Then he proceeds to give examples that help us understand the point he is making. He mentions three generations of the patriarchs, each of which demonstrates the fact that God is sovereign in salvation. First was Abraham, himself an example of the sovereign mercy of God, because when God called him, he was worshiping idols. Abraham did not choose God; rather, God chose Abraham. Then Abraham had two sons, Isaac and Ishmael, the next generation. Were they both saved? No, God told Abraham that his spiritual children would come only through Isaac. Although Ishmael was his biological child, he was not the one who had the promise of God. But not even Isaac could fully prove Paul's case of God's sovereign choice in salvation, because Ishmael's mother was an Egyptian. So maybe Isaac was chosen by this circumstance of birth. He was fully an Israelite.

But in verse 10, the example of the third generation clinches Paul's argument. The sons of Isaac, Jacob and Esau, not only had the same parents, but were also twins. How little there was to choose between them! And yet, as verse 11 points out, even before they were born, even before they had done anything right or wrong, God chose Jacob and not Esau. He discriminated between them. He gave Jacob preferential treatment, which is really what is meant when God speaks about loving Jacob and hating Esau (v. 13). The mercy that God showed to Jacob did not depend on his godliness. It did not depend on his birthright, either, because he was the second born. But he was the son of God's choice.

The meaning of these examples is unmistakable. Salvation is based not on anything in us, but only on the redeeming mercy of the sovereign God. It is that very reason that God gives for choosing Jacob: "that God's purpose in election might stand" (Rom. 9:11 NIV), in order that election might be demonstrated. God chose Jacob precisely to teach these mysteries of the sovereignty of God, that he is sovereign in the dispensation of his mercy. Even before birth, God predestines those who will receive his saving grace, and Jacob himself was chosen for the purpose of demonstrating that God's grace is God's choice.

Now as soon as we hear that, we may object, maybe holding forth the objection that Paul himself raises in verse 14. Even if election is biblical, even if God really is sovereign in the dispensation of his mercy, as it seems that Paul has just demonstrated with many biblical examples, we may still wonder whether that is really fair. That's exactly the objection that Paul expects people to make, which confirms that he really is teaching here the doctrine of the sovereignty of God in salvation. In fact, this passage deals with exactly the kinds of objections that people usually have against Reformed theology, as it is often called, or Calvinism. As soon as we say that salvation comes from the mercy of God, the first thing people are likely to think is that it's not fair.

These objections remind me of a story the late Dr. Edmund Clowney once told about an experience he had as a student at Wheaton College. He was in chapel, listening to somebody thoroughly critique any kind of Reformed theology. A thoroughly Arminian position was being developed in that chapel message, and as he was listening to the message, he was fairly persuaded by it. But he said to himself, "There is something very familiar about the objections that are being raised about the sovereignty of God and salvation." When he went back to his dorm room, it occurred to him all of a sudden: "I know where I have heard these objections before. I have heard them from the apostle Paul in Romans 9—not as the doctrine that Paul is articulating, but as the objection that Paul is raising to his own doctrine." That realization really gave Dr. Clowney something to think about.

If you share similar objections to God's sovereign mercy in redemption, that it doesn't seem fair, then you may be sure that the question you are raising is an objection to what the Bible really is teaching. Paul doesn't simply raise that objection, but he also answers it. Notice what a flat denial he gives in verse 14. Is God unjust? By no means, not at all! You might even say, "God forbid"—that's the strength of the expression that Paul is using here. And then, in order to justify God, Paul refers back to Exodus 33, where God says, "I will have mercy on whom I have mercy, and I will have compassion on whom I have compassion" (Rom. 9:15). God himself claims exactly the sovereignty that Paul has been asserting on his behalf. Is this doctrine of the sovereign mercy of God something that Paul is making up, or is it something that God has revealed all through the history of his people? "Well," Paul says, "just look at your Bible, which, of course, is the final authority for any doctrine. God himself claims the right to have mercy on whom he will have mercy." Apart from the counsel of God's own will, nothing determines for God the proper objects of his mercy.

Now does God's statement really answer the objection, or does it simply bring us back to the issue again? Just think about that for a moment. The objection is that God's sovereign mercy is unfair, that it is unjust for God to choose some, but not others. Yet it is very striking that, in his answer, Paul says nothing about justice at all. He speaks only about mercy. And that, I think, is actually the point. Salvation is not about something that is fair, because what is truly fair is for every sinner to be condemned to the wrath and curse of God. That's what the Scripture says about our sins. That's what I deserve. May I say that it is what you deserve as well? That's what the Scripture teaches about our sinful condition from birth and even before that. So, if we insist on fairness, then the question of mercy will never come up at all. The question of salvation will never come up, because no one will ever be saved.

But God is a merciful God, and his mercy is in a category entirely different from justice. In salvation, God is giving us not what we deserve, but what we could never deserve. It does not therefore depend on man's desire or effort (Rom. 9:16). It doesn't depend on human will or exertion, but on God who has mercy. This is the basis for our salvation, not anything that we could want or do.

What God said to Moses holds true for salvation in Christ. From beginning to end, it's all about the mercy of God. It's only by the mercy of God that you even hear the gospel and understand that there is a way of salvation. It's only by the mercy of God that you are able to believe in Jesus Christ and in his salvation. It's only by the mercy of God that you are justified, that he imputes to you the righteousness of Jesus Christ, so that you can stand righteous before God. It's only by the mercy of God that you are welcomed into the family of God and the Father says to you, "You are my beloved son; you are my beloved daughter." It's only by mercy that we are sanctified, made to be like Christ. It's only by mercy that one day we will be raised in glory and will become even more like Christ, conformed to his glorious image. Our whole redemption is just one mercy after another. It's all what God has done on our behalf, not what we could do or deserve. And all of it flows from the cross. This is where God has supremely demonstrated his mercy to sinners. Mercy is found in the life that Jesus offered for our sins. If you are a believer in Jesus Christ, you know deep down that this is true—that all of your salvation, every last bit of it, comes from God. It's all, then, to be returned to him in praise.

Even having said that our salvation is all because of his mercy, we naturally wonder about those who have not received God's mercy—or at least not yet. We wonder if they will be saved, and if not, why not? The Bible addresses this question by reminding us of Pharaoh: "'For this very purpose I have raised you up, that I might show my power in you, and that my name might be proclaimed in all the earth.' So then he has mercy on whomever he wills, and he hardens whomever he wills" (Rom. 9:17–18). Here Paul provides a test case of those who are passed by.

Here we confront what is a hard truth for us: that, while God shows mercy on some, he leaves others in their sins. If you wanted to give this situation a technical term, it's the doctrine of "reprobation," the flip side of election. Calvin noted that God rejects some persons to eternal condemnation, in a way parallel but opposite to the way that he ordains others to salvation. Now, is this fair? Yes, because in reprobation God gives sinners what they actually deserve. You have to remember that those who are passed by are not innocent, but are surely guilty, as was Pharaoh. He hated God and sought to destroy the people of God. Was it not fair for him to be judged for his sins and ultimately to perish? Yes, it was fair. Pharaoh had no one to blame but himself. God did not make Pharaoh sin any more than he makes anyone sin. But he did withhold his mercy from Pharaoh, according to the counsel of his own will. He let Pharaoh continue in his sins. Pharaoh was abandoned to his sins, while Moses was saved, simply because God will have mercy on whom he has mercy, as Scripture says.

Perhaps you would have developed the plan of salvation differently. But this is how God chose to save, and, of course, it is his sovereign right to do so. If we have trouble understanding these things, perhaps it will help us to go back and reckon with what the Bible teaches about what it really means to be dead in sin. If we are dead in sin apart from Christ, then any spiritual life has to come from God. It cannot come from ourselves. God does not owe his mercy to anyone, and so, unless he chooses to grant it, we will never be saved.

Shortly after the death of James Boice, we received a letter at my church from someone who wanted to thank him for his teaching on this topic of the sovereignty of the mercy of God. The writer himself had taught from Romans 9 and had suffered strong opposition on this very point of doctrine. The conflict reminded him of his own struggle at an earlier point of life to understand the sovereignty of God's mercy. When he had heard people speak about these things, he had been horrified. He tried to disprove that teaching and found that he could not accept it until he sat by the deathbed of his father. In his letter, he described the experience of being at his father's side, holding his hand while he took his final breath. Before calling the medical staff, he sat for some twenty minutes next to the lifeless body, and he wrote this about that experience:

> There was absolutely no life in that body, and I was helpless to do anything to change that fact. I began to think about Ephesians 2: We were dead in transgressions and sins. I began to think about Romans 9: The sinful mind cannot submit to God. It's hostile to God. I began to think about the teaching of the Bible, about election and the sovereignty of God. And for the first time in my life I understood the significance of it. I was overwhelmed by God's grace. Why would he choose me? I realized it was because he is sovereign, not because he saw anything in me, and I was overwhelmed by his grace.

Truly, the wonder of wonders is that God chooses to save anyone, and the name that we give to that wonder is mercy, the mercy of God for sinners who are unable to save themselves.

Now, Paul raises a second objection to God's sovereign mercy in salvation in verse 19: "You will say to me then, 'Why does he still find fault? For who can resist his will?'" Once again, this is precisely the kind of objection that is often raised against the sovereign and electing purpose of God in salvation. I think it confirms that Paul really is teaching this doctrine. This objection is based not on fairness, but on free will: if God's grace is God's choice, then there is nothing we can do about it. If we are not among the elect, it's not our fault. It's God's fault, and therefore we should not be held accountable. Here the paradox of divine sovereignty and human responsibility is introduced.

If Paul did not intend to teach what I have referred to as the doctrine of reprobation, this would have been the perfect place for him to explain himself and say, "No, don't misunderstand me. Our choice to reject God has nothing to do with his sovereignty." That's how he could have removed this objection. Yet that is not how he handles the objection at all.

Paul has little patience with this appeal to free will. Basically, he says that God is the Creator and we are his creatures. That reality gives God the right to do as he pleases. Incidentally, this relationship shows a very important connection: the sovereignty of God in creation is related to his sovereignty in salvation. When we think about God doing what he pleases, it's important to bear in mind that the creatures in question are sinful. At the end of this chapter, when Paul wants to explain why the Jews who have not believed in Christ are cut off from him, he does not say that they are cut off because they are not elect. He says that they are cut off because of their sins, because they do not believe in Jesus Christ. God doesn't judge people for not being elect, but for being sinners. In other words, no one has ever been condemned for not being chosen. We are condemned for not following after God and not trusting in Jesus Christ.

But even if we are willing to admit that God has the right to choose, we may still wonder why he has mercy on some and not on others. Perhaps if you had determined the plan of salvation, you would have had mercy on everyone. That's what some people expect that God should do. But, of course, God is not obligated to do that. In Romans 9:22–23, the Bible gives us at least the hint of an answer why he does not:

What if God, choosing to show his wrath and make his power known, bore with great patience the objects of his wrath—prepared for destruction? What if he did this to make the riches of his glory known to the objects of his mercy, whom he prepared in advance for glory? (NIV)

Paul's implication is that this is exactly what God has done. It was never his intention only to show mercy, as if that were the only attribute of God, but to demonstrate all his attributes, including his justice and even his wrath. God is as glorified in those attributes as he is in his mercy.

It has always been his intention to make a full display of his divine character. All through the Old Testament, God glorifies himself, not simply in salvation, but also in judgment. Even in the New Testament, whether you think about Ananias and Sapphira, Paul's condemnation of false teachers, or the judgments in the book of Revelation, God reveals himself as a God of mercy and also of justice and wrath. It's not arbitrary. It's not unjust. It is God's righteous way of dealing with sin. And in those contexts, typically what you will find is that praise is given to God for that very judgment, for that very justice is part of what deserves praise.

When God revealed the glory of his mercy to Moses (Ex. 33), he did not proclaim just his compassion and love, but also his justice and wrath. One testimony to God's glory is that he does not clear the guilty, but brings them under condemnation. Moses saw the fullness of God's revelation of his divine character in all his attributes. Just so, even here in election and reprobation, as in all his works, God does what he does because he is who he is. His aim is to show the glory of his sovereignty, his absolute independence, his right to do with his creatures as he pleases. What better way is there for God to show that he truly is sovereign than to show mercy to whom he will show mercy, and also to carry out justice in order to reveal his glory to those whom he has rescued from that justice! In both his justice and his mercy, there is something glorious about God, something godlike about him. He is demonstrating the divine character of his deity.

God's statement to Pharaoh in Exodus 9 is a perfect example. God was telling Pharaoh to let his people go, and Pharaoh was continuously refusing. Yet God came back to him again and again. Finally, God said, "I have raised you up for this very purpose, that I might show you my power and that my name might be proclaimed in all the earth" (Ex. 9:16 NIV). God acted as he did with Pharaoh so that he could glorify himself in all the earth. Do you know what the Israelites did when the Egyptians finally were destroyed? They didn't stand on the shores of the Red Sea arguing about the sovereignty of God, worrying about reprobation or its fairness. They glorified God because they had seen how glorious he was, not only in the mercy that he had shown to them, but also in the condemnation of sin and the way that he had brought justice. They were not trying to defend the sovereignty of God; they were simply celebrating it: "I will sing to the LORD, for he is highly exalted. The horse and its rider he has hurled into the sea. The LORD is my strength and my song; he has become my salvation" (Ex. 15:1–2 NIV).

Now, I want to close with several brief points of application. First, the only way to receive God's mercy instead of his wrath is to go to him and ask for it—to say, "God, be merciful to me, a sinner." This is the sinner's prayer in Luke 18:13. This is the appropriate response when we are confronted with the reality of God's justice and we wonder, "How can there be mercy for me?" God loves to show mercy.

The sinner's cry for mercy from the sovereign God can be well illustrated from the ministry of Benjamin Morgan Palmer.

In the 1840s, when revival was sweeping through Savannah, Georgia, a young man came to Palmer to complain about his Calvinism, his Reformed theology. "You preachers are the most contradictory men in the world," he said. "Why, yesterday you said in your sermon that sinners were perfectly helpless in themselves—utterly unable to repent or believe and then turned square round and said that they would all be dammed if they did not."[2]

Palmer sensed that his visitor was wrestling with the great issues of life and death, and he wanted to make sure that the man really dealt with the gospel, so he gave him a very indifferent response, kind of a brush-off. He said, "Well, my dear [sir], there is no use in our quarreling over this matter; either you can [believe in God] or you cannot. If you can, all I have to say is that I hope you will just go and do it."[3]

Then Palmer describes what happened next:

As I did not raise my eyes from my writing, which was continued as I spoke, I had no means of marking the effect of these words, until, after a moment's silence, with a choking utterance, the reply came back: "I have been trying my best for three whole days, and cannot." "Ah," said I, laying down the pen; "that puts a different face upon it; we will go then and tell the difficulty straight to God."

We knelt together and I prayed as though this was the first time in human history that this trouble had ever arisen; that here was a soul in the most desperate extremity, which must believe or perish, and hopelessly unable of itself, to do it; that, consequently it was just the case calling for Divine interposition. . . . Upon rising I offered not one single word of comfort or advice. . . . I left my friend in his powerlessness in

2. Quoted in Thomas Cary Johnson, *The Life and Letters of Benjamin Morgan Palmer* (Richmond: Presbyterian Committee of Publication, 1906), 83.
3. Ibid., 84.

the hands of God, as the only helper. In a short time he came through the struggle, rejoicing in the hope of eternal life.[4]

Here was a man, helpless in himself, saved by the sovereign mercy of God. There was nothing he could do to affect his own salvation, but he asked God to intervene, and God did, because he loves to show mercy to those who ask. That brings me to a second application. Palmer said that this man went on his way, rejoicing in the hope of eternal life. We too should worship God for his mercy, even for the sovereignty of his mercy. This is why God's grace must be his choice from beginning to end: so that he will receive all the glory, so that we will reserve nothing for ourselves but will say that it is all of God and of his grace, that it has all been his mercy upon mercy upon mercy, in order that all the praise might return to him.

Paul appropriately ends this section of Romans with worship. His argument for the sovereignty of God in salvation, his mercy in election, and his justice in reprobation builds through chapter 9, chapter 10, and chapter 11. Romans 11:32 concludes that God has bound all men over to disobedience, so that he may have mercy on them all, both Jews and Gentiles. But Paul doesn't end there. He doesn't end by saying, "These are really difficult problems of human responsibility and divine sovereignty, and I don't know how to fit them all together." Nor does he end by wringing his hands or despairing of ever being able to understand these things. No, he turns to praise; he bursts into song: "Oh, the depth of the riches of the wisdom and knowledge of God! How unsearchable his judgments" (v. 33 NIV). What an apt expression that is when you have been wrestling with questions pertaining to God's mercy and justice, his sovereignty in salvation!

4. Ibid.

"Who has known the mind of the Lord?
  Or who has been his counselor?"
"Who has ever given to God,
  that God should repay him?"
For from him and through him and to him are all things.
  To him be the glory forever! (Rom. 11:34–36 NIV)

Finally, we respond to the mercy of God by being merciful ourselves. I would be wrong not to include this application. Sadly, some people who believe in the sovereignty of God's mercy are not always known for their own mercy to others. It seems to me that someone who understands the wonder of God's mercy would seek to become a living demonstration of it. Remember what Jesus said: "Blessed are the merciful, for they will be shown mercy" (Matt. 5:7 NIV). We ought to be able to reverse that statement: "Blessed are those who have been shown mercy, for they will be merciful."

The test of our own grasp of the mercy of God is how we treat other sinners. How do you respond when you encounter a homeless person? How do you respond when you have an encounter with a gay prostitute on the street, or a drunk, or a coworker or family member or church member? How do I respond when I receive a profane tirade on the telephone? How do we respond in difficult circumstances? Often our response is anger. We wonder why those people can't get their act together. That's hardly the response of someone who knows the mercy of God, who understands that the bondage of sin is only ever broken through the mercy of the cross.

I have observed that some Christians are Calvinists when they deal with their own sins, but Arminians when it comes to others. They have learned that the only answer to their own depravity is divine grace. But somehow they seem to expect other people to save themselves. Now, certainly it's the case that God holds sinners responsible for their sins, but he is reaching out to them in mercy. If you understand the sovereignty of God in redemption, you will not be judgmental or proud, but you yourself will become a messenger of the mercy of God, for "what does the LORD require of you? To act justly and to love mercy and to walk humbly with your God" (Mic. 6:8 NIV).

6

Sanctifying Grace[1]

MICHAEL S. HORTON

WHAT DO YOU envision when you thank God for the atoning work of our Savior? Out of that work come many gifts, planned by the Father from all eternity and applied by the Holy Spirit. But how often, when we talk about sanctification, do we turn our attention away from Christ and the cross? How often do we mash our ideas of sanctification together with the twisted trends and worldviews of our culture? In order to truly understand the process of salvation that Paul describes in Romans 6–8, we first need to tug ourselves free from the misconceptions of our self-help and therapy-obsessed culture.

Maureen O'Hara and Walter Truett Anderson have recently underscored my growing suspicion that the therapeutic industry is in pretty bad shape these days. O'Hara introduces us to a few of her patients from her experience in San Diego—where you get a lot of work if you're a psychotherapist. I know, because I

1. Modified portions of this chapter appear in Michael S. Horton, "A New Creation," *Modern Reformation* 12, no. 3 (May–June 2003): 28–36.

live there. (The following names have been changed, of course, to prevent legal action.)

> Jerry feels overwhelmed, anxious, fragmented, and confused. He disagrees with people he used to agree with and aligns himself with people he used to argue with. He questions his sense of reality and frequently asks himself what it all means. He has had all kinds of therapeutic and growth experiences: Gestalt, rebirthing, Jungian analysis, holotropic breathwork, bioenergetics, "A Course in Miracles," twelve-step recovery groups, Zen meditation, Ericksonian hypnosis. He has been to sweat lodges, to the Rajneesh ashram in Poona, India, to the Wicca Festival in Devon. He is in analysis again, this time with a self-psychologist. Although he is endlessly on the lookout for new ideas and experiences, he keeps saying he wishes he could simplify his life. He talks about buying land in Oregon. He loved *Dances with Wolves*. Jerry is like so many educated professionals who come in for psychotherapy these days. But he is not quite the typical client: he is a well-established psychotherapist.
>
> Beverly comes into therapy torn between two lifestyles and two identities. In the California city where she goes to college, she is a radical feminist; on visits to her Midwestern hometown, she is a nice, sweet, square, conservative girl. The therapist asks her when she feels most like herself. She says, "When I'm on the airplane."[2]

Both of these people, O'Hara and Anderson write, are "shoppers in the great marketplace of realities. . . . Here a religion, there an ideology, over there a lifestyle."[3]

2. Maureen O'Hara and Walter Truett Anderson, "Psychotherapy's Own Identity Crisis," in *The Truth about the Truth: De-confusing and Re-constructing the Postmodern World*, ed. Walter Truett Anderson (New York: Putnam, 1995), 170.
    3. Ibid.

Another psychologist, Robert Jay Lifton, a pioneer in neuropsychology, has described this identity crisis as the "protean self,"[4] based on the ancient Greek myth of Proteus, a god who eluded capture by changing himself into different shapes. Lifton says that that is exactly what the postmodern self is all about: constant transformation, makeovers, I need a new me. I'm tired of this identity; I want a new one; I'm bored with my life. What in the earlier part of his career was considered personality disorder, Lifton says, is now considered normal.

Some years ago, Nordstrom had a campaign built on this trend: "Reinvent Yourself." This self-transformation is what our culture is obsessed with. When our culture hears us talking about redemption, and certainly when our culture hears us talking about sanctification, they mean this type of therapy. They mean "Help to massage my ego" or "Help to give me a different identity that I will like this time."

But this type of help is not sanctification. Instead, Jesus comes not to help us, but to kill us, so that he can make us alive in him. Ecclesiastes reminds us that, "under the sun," all is vanity. "Vanity of vanities," said the man who had it all. So we go to the marketplace of identities, from booth to booth at Vanity Fair, finally asking, "Is that all there is? Do you have anything more?" And the more we reinvent ourselves, the more protean we become in our identities, the more we are actually running from the one Person who can chain us and tell us who we really are. Like Proteus, we keep doing this business in order to evade capture. We're Adam and Eve running from God, sewing fig leaves to cover our nakedness, as if God couldn't see through that. But we don't seem to care what God thinks. The important thing to us is, "Can I live with myself with these fig leaves?"

4. See Robert Jay Lifton, "The Protean Style," in ibid., 130–35.

Modern religion is all about getting the right fig leaves and putting them on nicely, making sure they are decorative and that other people know that they're there.

But the truth is that our bodies are aging; we are dying today. Every one of us is dying. Our charisma is fading. Our minds are forgetful—or, too often, are so distracted by the trivial that, as C. S. Lewis said, we're like children making mud pies instead of having a holiday at the sea.[5] We don't know what it's like to glorify God and enjoy him forever. We don't really know what it's like to have all of our fulfillment and satisfaction and identity in Jesus Christ.

But it is into this world and this present age that the age to come, the kingdom of God, comes to us. Into our culture of restless change and obsessive narcissism, into this world that is not simply twenty-first-century America, but the way we've been since Adam, an announcement comes from another world, proclaiming something that has happened outside of us, something done for us by someone else in history that anchors our identity outside of ourselves. This event does not give us a "new me," does not improve the self, does not ask, "What would you like to be today? Are you an autumn or a summer?" Rather, it says, "Forget you—I am going to tell you what I did for you. Pull your head out of yourself." Augustine defined the essence of sin as being curved in on ourselves. We are so bent over that all we can see is the ground beneath us. So we make the ground pretty; we make everything delightful, and we think we have improved the real world. But the gospel comes to us and says, "Oh, you poor, small soul! Look outside of yourself. I will bend you back, so you can see the whole vista that you've never seen before."

5. C. S. Lewis, *The Weight of Glory* (1949; repr., New York: HarperCollins, 2001), 26.

God doesn't blame us for having desires that are too strong, said Lewis, but for passions that are too weak.[6] We play around with trivial things and bypass the best. But into this restless turbulence of changing identity, Paul brings the gospel in Romans 6—not only of justification, but of renewal in Christ:

> What then are we to say? Should we continue in sin in order that grace may abound? By no means! How can we who died to sin go on living in it? Do you not know that all of us who have been baptized into Christ Jesus were baptized into his death? Therefore we have been buried with him by baptism into death, so that, just as Christ was raised from the dead by the glory of the Father, so we too might walk in newness of life.
>
> For if we have been united with him in a death like his, we will certainly be united with him in a resurrection like his. (vv. 1–5 NRSV)

Did our old self simply have a makeover? No, we know that "our old self was crucified with him so that the body of sin might be destroyed" (v. 6 NRSV)—not merely helped—and that we might no longer be enslaved by sin.

> For whoever has died is freed from sin. But if we have died with Christ, we believe that we will also live with him. We know that Christ, being raised from the dead, will never die again; death no longer has dominion over him. The death he died, he died to sin, once for all; but the life he lives, he lives to God. So you also must consider yourselves dead to sin and alive to God in Christ Jesus.
>
> Therefore, do not let sin exercise dominion in your mortal bodies, to make you obey their passions. No longer present

6. Ibid.

your members to sin as instruments of wickedness, but present yourselves to God as those who have been brought from death to life, and present your members to God as instruments of righteousness. For sin will have no dominion over you, since you are not under law but under grace. (vv. 7–14 NRSV)

What an amazing announcement! Just when you thought that the gospel had exhausted itself, there is more. The gospel liberates us not only from the guilt and penalty of sin, but from the power and dominion of sin as well.

The argument that Paul unfolds in this section of Roman 6 plays an important part in the unfolding argument of the two Adams and the time that we live in redemptive history. After concluding in Romans 3:9–20 that the whole world stands condemned by God's law, either on the basis of the law written on the conscience in creation or on the basis of the law written on tablets of stone, Paul proclaims that everyone knows God's expectations. We know God's moral will. We don't know his saving will apart from his telling us, but we don't need a special revelation to tell us what God's moral will is for our lives. It's amazing how the Code of Hammurabi parallels the Ten Commandments. The code of loving God and loving your neighbor is amazingly universal. If you speak to people who have never been raised in the church, people from all kinds of different religious backgrounds, they will agree that religion is all about loving God and loving your neighbor.

But things start to get dicey when you start talking about Jesus as the only way, truth, and life—when you speak of the cross and the resurrection, the particulars of the Christian faith that divide the whole human race. Why? Because the gospel is what we don't know by nature. It doesn't unite us; it divides us into believers and unbelievers. But even if we haven't heard the gospel, we suppress the truth in unrighteousness. We suppress the law, push it down, distort it, twist it. But God says that on the last day, everyone will be judged by his law.

Now the question is this: how is God going to save anybody without violating his justice? What if God walked into the courtroom and said, "I'll let bygones be bygones. You know, boys will be boys. I'm going to overlook your sin because I'm a nice God. I'm a God of love, not a God of justice and wrath, so I'm going to turn and look the other way"? As the Bible's depiction of his justice clearly shows, he can't do that. His justice must be satisfied; his wrath must be assuaged. So God has swept the whole human race into one lost heap and put the sign "condemned" over it. No part of humanity can pull itself away from God's wrath.

In that one place where everyone stands condemned by the law, Jew and Gentile alike, everyone is now ready to hear the gospel that is for everyone, Jew and Gentile alike. That's the great news: there is both a righteousness of God that damns us (the law) and a righteousness from God that saves us (justification). God gives as a free gift the righteousness that he demands in the law. He gives this free gift, not by pouring it into us, not by giving us a little bit at a time, not by infusing it like an IV into our spiritual veins. It is a courtroom verdict that stands, despite the fact that our every thought and action seems to be evidence against it. God declares us righteous while we are actually unrighteous in ourselves. That is the scandal of Christianity. That is the foolishness of the cross. That's why everybody from Oprah and Dr. Phil to countless preachers across America will not tell that story, even if they talk about Jesus. That radical concept ruins religion completely. It unleashes us for the first time to really be freely obedient in Christ, but that's not the same as religion or public morality. Public morality is important, but it's not sanctification.

No subjective condition of our hearts, no doubt in our minds, no affliction of our bodies, Paul says, will ever be able to change what God has already done. He has already chosen us in Christ. He has already redeemed us by Christ, and he has already called us into fellowship and union with his Son by his Spirit. He has given us the Holy Spirit as a pledge, a down payment, a deposit that guarantees our final resurrection. But all the righteousness that we have right now before God's throne belongs to someone else. It is Christ's righteousness imputed to us by faith alone, apart from works. That's the radical part of gospel.

It's true, according to Romans, that where sin abounds, grace abounds all the more. So we think, "Hmmm, I could get used to this. I like to sin; God likes to forgive. It's a perfect match." So shall we go on living in sin so that grace may abound? Imagine the responses that we might give to that question today. On the one hand, there is the pop culture response: "Don't worry about it. Your good outweighs your bad. Deep down, you're a good person." On the other hand, there is the more rigorous approach to the question: "If you continue to sin, do you lose your salvation? Do you lose your rewards? You may be saved, but singed. You'll just get in by the skin of your teeth. You'll make it because of eternal security, but you're not going to have many crowns." One proponent of the latter view oddly argues that the place of weeping and wailing and gnashing of teeth is actually reserved for carnal Christians. They will be saved, but will inhabit the Third World part of heaven.[7]

What is Paul's answer? "Shall we continue in sin, that grace may abound? God forbid" (Rom. 6:1–2 KJV). He says neither "You better not . . . or else," nor "Oh, don't worry about it." Paul's response is neither legalism nor antinomianism. Paul says, "Stop

7. See Charles Stanley, *Eternal Security: Can You Be Sure?* (Nashville: Thomas Nelson, 1990), 124–26.

looking at yourself. Look at Christ. Do you have any concept of what has happened to you? Haven't you figured out the gospel yet? You died; your life is hidden with God in Christ. That's who you are now. You're not an autonomous little god, using God when you feel like he might be helpful. That person was put to death. That person has been buried in baptism and has been raised in newness of life." The real differences are not between carnal Christians and victorious Christians, but between those who are in Adam and those who are in Christ. All who are in Adam are dead—not unwell, but dead. All who are in Christ are saved, elect, justified, regenerated, redeemed new creatures in Jesus Christ.

Union with Christ is both federal and organic. What does *federal* mean? Every election cycle we hear a lot about *federal* this, *federal* that. Federal government actually in many ways came out of the federal theology of the Reformed tradition. It began as a theological idea—representative government. Just as we elect officials to represent us in government, Christ has pledged himself to be the mediator and head of his people. And so throughout Romans 5, Paul talks about the two heads of two covenants, the covenant of works and the covenant of grace:

> Therefore, just as sin came into the world through one man, and death came through sin, and so death spread to all because all have sinned—sin was indeed in the world before the law, but sin is not reckoned when there is no law. . . .
>
> But the free gift is not like the trespass. For if the many died through the one man's trespass, much more surely have the grace of God and the free gift in the grace of the one man, Jesus Christ, abounded for the many. And the free gift is not like the effect of the one man's sin. For the judgment following one trespass brought condemnation, but the free gift following many trespasses brings justification. If, because of the one man's trespass, death exercised dominion through that

one, much more surely will those who receive the abundance of grace and the free gift of righteousness exercise dominion in life through the one man, Jesus Christ. . . .

For just as by the one man's disobedience the many were made sinners, so by the one man's obedience the many will be made righteous. But law came in, with the result that the trespass multiplied; but where sin increased, grace abounded all the more, so that, just as sin exercised dominion in death, so grace might also exercise dominion through justification leading to eternal life through Jesus Christ our Lord. (vv. 12–13, 15–17, 19–21 NRSV)

Justification outran sin, and that's what leads to the question that Paul knows we're all wondering about: should we then continue in sin? He answers clearly: "No, of course not. Don't you remember that you are in Christ? Federally, he is your representative head. You are justified in him."

On the other hand, we're also organically united to Jesus Christ. To depict this relationship, we move out of the language of the courtroom and into the language of biology: a vine and its branches, a tree and its fruit, a head and its body. These are organic images. As Adam's heirs, it is impossible for us to bear any fruit other than Adamic fruit. That doesn't mean that all of the works of those in Adam are unhelpful for humanity or as bad as they could possibly be. We produce some civil righteousness—that is, righteousness before human beings that they can respect. But it all produces the same fruit of death. However, in Christ as the covenantal head, we not only have the legal imputation of his righteousness, but also actually have his life flowing through us, coursing through our spiritual veins, bearing fruit that will last. That's Paul's point here.

This organic life is also what Jesus spoke of in John 15:16: "You did not choose me but I chose you. And I appointed you to go and bear fruit, fruit that will last" (John 15:16 NRSV). Have hope! What a difference! Instead of being berated Sunday after Sunday for not having enough fruit, we have hope in this organic connection. In the world, anyone can say, "Are you producing fruit? Well, go out and do it." Any self-help program can give advice: Suze Orman for your finances, Jake to improve your body. You don't need God for that kind of religion. But we Christians know that we are destitute. We cry out, "O wretched man that I am! Who will deliver me from this body of death?" (Rom. 7:24 NKJV). And, consequently, we have Christ working in us by his Spirit, pledged to us unconditionally by God through his gospel. Our sanctification is definitive, once-and-for-all separation from the mass of condemned humanity and separation unto God. It's a once-and-for-all holiness, so that Paul can say in 1 Corinthians 1:30 that Christ is our holiness—not only our justification, but also our sanctification.

Yet Scripture also talks about our working out sanctification in a progressive way throughout our whole life. It's important that we remember the progressive sanctification that marks our lives, the progressive war with indwelling sin, which is the working out of that verdict that we have already received in justification. Justification is once and for all. Justification is not progressive—but it takes a long time to get used to being declared righteous when you know you're not. The process that God works in us in this age is sanctification—progressively making us look more like that which he already declares us to be and that which we will perfectly be when we're glorified.

At the beginning of Romans 6, Paul isn't issuing a command. He's making an announcement. This declaration puts wind in our sails. We've got to stop talking about the freedom of the gospel when we talk about justification, while putting people back under bondage when we talk about sanctification.

The whole process is under the gospel. Even for the Christian, the law always tells us what God expects of us, but it cannot get us to perform it. The law is the instrument that tells us where to go and when we're lost, but the instruments on a sailboat can't move it along. Movement requires wind. The gospel is that wind in our sails. That's why Paul proclaims that grace gets better than justification. God is so good and so gracious that he has not only taken away our curse—he has also taken away the dominion of sin in our life.

That is certainly good news. What terrible rescuers would save you from the imminent destruction of a tyrant, only to leave you to be torn apart, limb by limb? Christ doesn't do that. Christian warfare is rated on the basis of Christ's victory, not on the basis of our own puny battles. Remember that you're in Christ. You died with him. Talk about him; find your life hidden in him. He died, and he is raised. It's not simply a matter of believing that something happened two thousand years ago. No, that death and resurrection is where your life is.

Has it really hit us—the sure objectivity of our salvation? It is a finished thing. Christ won the war. Now what we have are guerilla battles. Satan is really mad because he lost, so the battle looks more dangerous than it really is. Satan may be angry, but he is on a leash, and he knows that his time is near.

In the face of this great salvation, what defines you—the world of CNN, a fashion, entertainment, consumerism, being a blue American or a red American? What is your real world—this passing evil age, or the age to come that is breaking in with all of its glory, but is dismissed as irrelevance, unimportance, and foolishness in the eyes of the world? As believers, we all find our identity and home in Christ and his kingdom. There is no distinction between first-class and second-class Christians. All Christians are victorious Christians.

Finally, in Romans 7, Paul balances this knowledge of our present salvation with the "not yet" aspect. In typical rabbinical style, he moves back and forth between extremes, keeping us from going off the deep end on either side: "Does this mean that . . . ? No, here is the hedge on the other side." At first hearing, Romans 7 sounds like Paul is taking away with the right hand everything he gave with the left. He has just told us that sin cannot have dominion over us. He proclaims that every time we are presented with temptation, we can say, "I am in Christ; sin doesn't have a right to tell me what to do anymore. It's a toothless tiger. Why should I live as though something horrible were true, when it's really not?"

And yet, Romans 7 reminds us, we continue to sin. Why does Paul feel the need to stick this "downer" in the midst of all this good news? Many Christians today want to live in Romans 6 or in Romans 8—victorious and free. However, Paul is saying that all Christians simultaneously live in Romans 6, 7, and 8 at every moment in their Christian lives. We are simultaneously victorious and miserable, for "that which I want to do, I don't do, and that which I don't want to do, I keep on doing" (see 7:15). A lot of Christians have real trouble believing that this is Paul's personal experience. They think that no Christian could possibly see life as this horrible. But Paul says, "With my mind, I love the law" (see 7:22), something that no unbeliever does. He is describing not only himself, but the normal Christian, loving God's Word and desiring to obey its commands—but failing. That's our misery and our problem.

The gospel gives us a new desire: to obey the law. Sometimes people come to me and say, "I don't think I'm a Christian—I keep falling into this particular sin. I know I don't have a right to do that. That's why I don't think I am a Christian." But that's the best evidence I can imagine for their being a Christian.

Non-Christians don't worry about falling into sin. On the other hand, Paul points out that Christians are miserable over their sin, because they are now defined by the age to come and yet are living in opposition to it. There's crisis; there's conflict—that is the Christian life. As the age to come and this present age meet on the battlefield in your heart, your life, your family, your community, your church—Romans 7 validates that and reminds us of the "not yet" of our salvation.

The eighteenth-century Scottish Presbyterian minister Alexander Whyte used to squelch any holiness-perfectionist ideas by pointing down from his high pulpit and saying, "As long as you're under my charge, you'll never leave Romans 7." The slow growth and struggle might get really mundane over the rest of your life, but you're going to grow. You may not perceive it, but others will.

Yes, you'll never leave Romans 7, but you'll also never leave Romans 6. Both are true simultaneously for all of us believers. So let's not carve Christians into two groups or our Christian lives into two periods: one based on Romans 6, and one on Romans 7. We're all in Romans 6, and we're all in Romans 7—and, finally, we're all in Romans 8.

What accounts for the ups and downs in this section of Romans? In Romans 6, Paul has wind in his sails and is sailing out into the ocean blue. Why? He is looking to Christ, talking about being found in Christ. Then, in Romans 7, he starts talking about himself. The wind dies down, and he finds himself with a lot of good equipment and no place to go. In Romans 8, what fills his sails again? "Thanks be to God through Jesus Christ our Lord! . . . There is therefore now no condemnation for those who are in Christ Jesus" (7:25–8:1).

Romans 8 brings us back around to the reality that what the law could not do, God did—and that's not just for our justification, but for our sanctification as well. But he goes on to say that this progression gets even better: salvation is not just for our souls, but also for our bodies. The gospel is this: justification, and then sanctification as progressive, inward renewal, and one day an outward renewal. While the outer man is wasting away and decaying, the inner man is being renewed day by day. Right now, the outward contradicts the inward, but one day they'll match up. One day our bodies will be outwardly beautiful, outwardly vigorous, outwardly radiant with the glory of God, healthy and holy. The outer person and the inner person will be totally integrated on the day of resurrection. Not just our souls, but our total person will be saved by grace.

What's more, God will restore not just the total person, but the whole creation—which even now is groaning, waiting for the sons of God to be revealed—will be released from its bondage:

> For I consider that the sufferings of this present time are not worth comparing with the glory that is to be revealed to us. For the creation waits with eager longing for the revealing of the sons of God. For the creation was subjected to futility, not willingly, but because of him who subjected it, in hope that the creation itself will be set free from its bondage to corruption and obtain the freedom of the glory of the children of God. For we know that the whole creation has been groaning together in the pains of childbirth until now. And not only the creation, but we ourselves, who have the firstfruits of the Spirit, grown inwardly as we wait eagerly for adoption as sons, the redemption of our bodies. For in this hope we were saved. Now hope that is seen is not hope. For who hopes for what he sees? But if we hope for what we do not see, we wait for it with patience. (8:18–25)

That's the goal that keeps us restlessly moving—not as tourists in this world, but as pilgrims, not yet having arrived, but knowing where we're going. It's that kind of good restlessness that keeps us moving forward to that which lies ahead, realizing that we haven't arrived yet.

Acknowledging this truth is a realistic approach to the Christian life. We're all simultaneously in the justification of Romans 6, the incomplete sanctification of Romans 7, and the hope and anticipation of Romans 8. Through this process, God has pulled us outside of ourselves to look to Christ for salvation and to our neighbor for service.

7

Our Holy Redeemer

RICHARD D. PHILLIPS

WHILE ALL OF the Bible is God-breathed, certain portions are especially beloved in different ways—perhaps the great pastoral Psalm 23, the doxology of Psalm 19, or the treatise on the doctrine of salvation in Romans 8. Hebrews 7 isn't often mentioned among these great chapters. However, I want to make the case for Hebrews 7 as a great chapter on Christology, the person and work of our Lord Jesus Christ. This chapter forms a doctrinal staircase on Christology, climbing ever higher until the summary statement in verses 26–28, the passage that I will ultimately focus on.

Before we reach that pinnacle, however, let me bring us up to speed on the rest of the chapter. In verses 1–10, the author begins with Melchizedek as a type of Jesus Christ. Melchizedek shows the excellence of Christ as both king and priest, a bearer of righteousness and peace, displayed back in Genesis. As Abraham came to Melchizedek after his battles to acclaim him and be vindicated, Melchizedek nourished him with bread and wine.

So also our great high priest, the Lord Jesus, says to us, "Come to Me, all you who labor and are heavy laden, and I will give you rest" (Matt. 11:28 NKJV). From this comparison of Jesus to Melchizedek, Hebrews 7:11–19 argues that Jesus is a better hope than that found in the old covenant. The great overarching, pastoral purpose of the writer of Hebrews is that his Jewish-Christian readers not be tempted or persecuted into going back into the old covenant, so he often shows how Jesus is better than what was before. Here he argues that, when Jesus appears as the new priest, he brings with him a new administration of salvation that is better than what Israel had previously experienced. He argues that because Jesus possesses an indestructible life, he is able to give us life, so that we might have a better and firmer hope. Finally, Hebrews 7:20–25 informs us of the implications of Jesus' eternal and permanent priesthood, which he has because he lives forever. He is the guarantee of God's covenant.

As people unfamiliar with monarchy and priesthood, we often don't really appreciate the significance of the fact that Jesus lives forever. Back in the time when Hebrews was written, after the death of a king, everyone would wonder what the new king would be like. A good priest would die, and people wondered how the new priest would fulfill his office. On the other hand, Jesus reigns forever, and so he is able to assure and guarantee our salvation. The book of Hebrews gives a sense of the present, living, and everlasting ministry of the exalted priest and king, the Lord Jesus Christ. He is living, reigning now and always, securing our salvation. Through this permanence, according to verse 25, "he is able to save to the uttermost those who draw near to God through him." This is the wonderful news of Christology.

Finally, the climax of Hebrews 7 focuses on our holy Redeemer in a summation that forms one of the high points of the entire book of Hebrews: "It was indeed fitting that we should have such a high priest" (v. 26). Christ is not just admirable, not merely worthy in some abstract way. Rather, as the New International Version very helpfully puts it, "Such a high priest meets our need." He is perfectly fitting for us in his person and work, perfectly suited for our predicament, and perfectly able to save us to the uttermost. I think a better translation would say this: "Such a high priest was fitted to us." You see, the point is that he is perfectly suited to the work and office to which God has appointed him as high priest. He is appropriate in every way to be the holy Redeemer of sinful humankind. A helpful way to delve into this concept of "high priest" is to reflect upon the nature of a sacrifice. The ancient writer Herveus very helpfully points out that when one is discussing a sacrifice, there are four things to keep in mind, "namely: what is offered as a sacrifice, to whom the sacrifice is offered, by whom the sacrifice is offered, and for whom the sacrifice is offered."[1] We have already addressed two of these issues: for whom the sacrifice is offered (sinful mankind under the condemnation of the law), and to whom it is offered (the holy God, who is right to judge lost and sinful mankind). These two points describe our predicament: our unworthiness and condemnation in the presence of a God who is holy, holy, holy.

So what remains is the remedy, and that's what we are focusing on. Jesus is fitted to be the remedy by providing the answer for the last two considerations: what is offered and by whom the sacrifice is offered. That is, Jesus Christ is perfectly fitted to be our high priest in terms of the sacrifice he offers and the high priest he is in offering that sacrifice. As theologian John Owen says, "Unholy sinners stand in need of a holy priest, and

1. Quoted in John Owen, *Hebrews* (Wheaton, IL: Crossway, 1988), 178.

a holy sacrifice. What we have not in ourselves we must have in him, or we shall not be accepted with the Holy God, who is of purer eyes than to behold iniquity."[2] Such a high priest is the Lord Christ.

In light of this sacrificial context, the final section of Hebrews 7 sets Jesus forth as a high priest who is fitted to our need in that he offers himself as the sacrifice. Hebrews 7:26 says five things about Jesus as the sacrifice, beginning with a triplet of adjectives: *holy*, *innocent*, and *unstained*. All three point to the perfect holiness of Christ. Anglican clergyman Philip Hughes organizes these characteristics as, first, pertaining to God (he is holy); second, pertaining to other people (he is blameless); and third, pertaining to himself (he is pure).[3] Another commentator, William Lane, sees these adjectives as pertaining to Christ's various qualifications for the priesthood. He claims that they speak first to the religious qualification of a priest: he must be holy in the sense of "devout," referring to how Christ appears before God. Second, they address the moral qualification of a priest: Jesus was blameless, never having done wrong to his fellow men, sinless in his intention and in his actions. Finally, they speak to the cultic or professional qualification of a priest: Christ is pure, undefiled for priestly service.[4] Jesus is not merely pure in an external way, as the Pharisees thought of purity with their cleansing rituals, but he is pure throughout, outwardly and inwardly. By his holiness, blamelessness, and purity, Jesus qualifies as both the sacrifice and the high priest we need.

2. John Owen, *An Exposition of the Epistle to the Hebrews: With the Preliminary Exercitations*, vol. 3, rev. Edward Williams (London: T. Pitcher, 1790), 365–66.

3. See Philip Edgcumbe Hughes, *A Commentary on the Epistle to the Hebrews* (Grand Rapids: Eerdmans, 1977), 278.

4. See William Lane, *Hebrews: A Call to Commitment* (Nashville: Thomas Nelson, 1985; repr., Vancouver: Regent College Publishing, 2004), 112.

Next, the verse provides two participial phrases in a couplet: he is separated from sinners and exalted above the heavens. In what sense was Jesus separated or set apart from sinners? Owen answers nicely:

> He was not set apart from them in nature, "for God sent his own Son in the likeness of sinful men" (Romans 8:3), and he was not set apart from men during his ministry. He spoke with tax collectors and prostitutes and was rebuked for doing that. No, being set apart from sinners declares what Christ is, in his state and condition: he is holy. He is undefiled. He was separate from sin, its nature, causes, and effects, and he had to be holy to be our Redeemer. He became the middle person between God and sinners and so had to be separate from those sinners in the aspect for which he took their place. So our Lord Jesus went through life experiencing all manner of temptation and yet separate from sin. In this respect he is in a different category from sinful man.[5]

Notice that when the New Testament writers talk about the full humanity of Christ, they make the qualification "without sin." That sinlessness does not make him less human, but makes him more human. When people ask, "How can he be truly human if he has never sinned?" they fail to understand what true humanity was designed to be. He is all that we are not, but need to be, and so he offered himself for us.

My dear late pastor, James Montgomery Boice, nicely came to this point in his sermon, "Where Is the Lamb?" This question is asked in Genesis 22:7 by Isaac, Abraham's son, whom God has directed Abraham to sacrifice at the top of Mount Moriah. As Abraham and Isaac head toward the mountain, Isaac does

5. Owen, *Hebrews* (1988), 179.

not know that he is the one to be sacrificed. I often think of this son, kindling strapped to his back, walking up the hill. As they reach the top of the mountain, he asks his father, "Where is the lamb?" Abraham, trusting God despite his great anguish, answers his son by saying, "God will provide for himself the lamb for a burnt offering" (v. 8). And that's just what happens. As Abraham raises the knife to plunge it into Isaac's breast, an angel appears saying, "Abraham, Abraham! . . . Do not lay your hand on the boy . . . for now I know that you fear God, seeing you have not withheld your son, your only son, from me" (vv. 11–12). Abraham looks up, sees a ram caught in the thicket, and offers that ram as a sacrifice in Isaac's place. Thenceforth, Abraham names the place "the LORD will provide" (v. 14).

In his sermon, Dr. Boice points out that Isaac's question might well be the theme verse for the whole Old Testament: "Where is the lamb?" From Eden on, this great question was on the hearts of God's people until the coming of Christ. As early as Genesis 3, we learn that sinful man is clothed by God through the death of a lamb. When Adam and Eve sinned and received the curse, God slew innocent animals in their place (Gen. 3:21) and clothed them with the skins. How horrified they must have been to see a death taking place for the very first time, right before their eyes—an awful indicator that the wages of sin is death. Sinful man must either be judged or have another lay down an atoning sacrifice for him.

Apparently, Adam and Eve learned the way of salvation from God's teaching through this example, because they taught their son Abel to approach God only on the basis of a blood sacrifice. Both Abel and Cain brought sacrifices—Abel from his sheep, Cain from the fruit of the ground. Cain brought a picture of the work of his hands, while Abel brought a picture of an atoning sacrifice, the blood of the lamb. God's fateful, critical response to

Cain's sacrifice, even before Cain murdered Abel, was, "Where is the lamb?"

Later, in the time of Moses, this question became even more pronounced. To release the nation of Israel from Egypt, God broke Pharaoh's will by sending the angel of death, who slew all the Egyptian firstborn. Only the Israelites who had their doors marked by the blood of the Passover lamb escaped this judgment: "For I will pass through the land of Egypt that night, and I will strike all the firstborn in the land of Egypt. . . . The blood shall be a sign for you, on the houses where you are. And when I see the blood, I will pass over you, and no plague will befall you to destroy you, when I strike the land of Egypt" (Ex. 12:12–13). As the Israelites commemorated that night years afterwards, they must have reflected on the wailing of the Egyptian parents who had failed to provide a satisfactory answer to the angel's question: "Where is the lamb?"

Later on, when God was angry with Israel for their sin at Mount Sinai during the golden calf incident, Moses tried to intercede on their behalf. He wanted to placate God's wrath by paying for their sin himself, but God refused him. Why? Because Moses was not fitted to that: unqualified and unholy, he needed someone to atone for his own sins. The question is then raised: if even Moses was not holy enough to make such atonement, then "where is the Lamb?"

Eventually, Israel's priesthood was established and the sacrifice of lambs was institutionalized. My friend Robert Godfrey preached at my church in Florida a few years ago after he visited the Holy Land exhibit in Orlando. I will never forget his comments on the tabernacle there. He reported that they had a replica in perfect accordance with the Bible, except for one thing: no flies, no stench, no entrails. During the Passover in Jerusalem, rivers of blood would flow. It was the most amazing bloodletting you could imagine. But the need to repeat this ritual annually revealed that mere animals could not ultimately remove the stain of guilt. "Where is the lamb?"

Centuries later, upon the very rock where Abraham had made his altar and raised a knife above the breast of his son, Solomon built the Jewish temple (2 Chron. 3:1). There sacrifices were made century after century, day after day, all of them pointing forward to the true sacrifice that would someday be made on nearby Mount Calvary. On that day, unlike when Abraham sought to slay and offer his only beloved son, Isaac, no angel stayed the hand of God as hammers drove nails into the hands and feet of his Son. When he was crucified to atone for all the sins of all God's people, holy and therefore perfectly fitted for what he was doing, the Son of God answered once and for all the age-old question, "Where is the lamb?"

If Abraham had been present at Calvary, I think he would have thought back to his own time on the mount and remembered what God said to him through the angel: "Now I know that you fear God, seeing you have not withheld your son, your only son, from me." Surely Abraham would have replied to God, "Now I know that you love me, since you have not withheld your Son, your only Son, from me." Calvary was the answer to the anxious anticipation of the Old Testament question, "Where is the lamb?" As John the Baptist said, Jesus Christ, the holy Redeemer, is "the Lamb of God, who takes away the sin of the world" (John 1:29). As Jesus rode into Jerusalem on Palm Sunday, hundreds of thousands of Passover lambs were shepherded in for slaughter as well—a vivid association anticipating the cross. As Paul says in 1 Corinthians 5:7, "Christ, our Passover lamb, has been sacrificed." In Hebrews 7:26–28, we learn why Jesus alone is qualified to be this lamb. He is fitted to our need because he is holy, innocent, unstained, separate from sinners, and now exalted above the heavens. There his blood causes God's wrath to pass over us, as lamb's blood once did for the enslaved sons of Israel.

We began by noting four considerations for a sacrifice to be acceptable, each of which has been demonstrated in Christ. First, those for whom the sacrifice is offered are sinners like us. Second, the sacrifice is offered to the holy God of the universe. Third, Jesus is the perfectly fitted sacrifice. That leaves one final question: who will offer the sacrifice? The holy Redeemer, the Lord Jesus, who as the high priest of God's people is fitted to our needs in his priestly work—not only as the sacrifice, but also as the ministering priest in the presence of God.

In Hebrews 7:27, Jesus' high priestly work is contrasted with that of the Old Testament priests: "He has no need, like those high priests, to offer sacrifices daily, first for his own sins and then for those of the people." Those Israelite priests were not really able to meet our need. They were like someone who is hired for the job, is given the right tools, and works hard, but simply lacks the skill and qualifications to do the job. Sculptors need artistic ability, scientists need mathematical prowess, athletes need speed and strength, and priests need holiness. The nature of their work requires bringing the sacrifice to atone for sins into the holy presence of God, but the Levitical priests showed their inability at this precise point, because they first had to offer sacrifices for themselves.

On top of their lack of qualification, the priests' work was never done. The insufficiency of any one sacrifice was illustrated by the need for another to follow. On the other hand, in the greatest possible contrast, we read that Jesus sacrificed once for all when he offered himself up. Whereas those priests were sinners, he is holy. While their sacrifices were insufficient, his is sufficient. Whereas the Old Testament priests were unable to meet the needs of sinners, he is able once for all to reconcile us to God. Jesus alone is qualified.

In retrospect, more than one question should have nagged Old Testament believers. They should have asked not only, "Where is the lamb?" but also, "Where is the true priest?" Just as a sheep was unable to atone for human sin, so also a mortal priest, a sinner himself, was not qualified to bring the offering before God. Exodus 28 shows the great lengths to which priests needed to go in order to appear righteous and holy before God. This chapter describes the special garments made for the high priest: a breastplate, an ephod (a robe with a tunic), a turban, a sash. These garments were all made of gold and the finest linen. The colors of their decorations corresponded to the decorations of the tabernacle, so that the priest would fit in before God. In that garb, the priest displayed the resplendence of a holy high priest, but the very need for that outerwear vividly showed that the priest himself lacked the holiness that such ministry required.

A similar analogy works today: if you need the right clothes to be confident, you are not really confident. The priest needed holiness to be confident before God, and the fact that he had to put something on to have that confidence shows that he had no basis in himself for that confidence. Indeed, the Old Testament's accounts of the high priest remind me of a children's pageant. One child comes out as a sunflower, waving at his parents behind a little cardboard outfit, and then out comes another who is the sun, and still others follow behind with their cardboard cloud costumes, and then the little raindrops come dropping out. When the show's over, everybody applauds. Just so, the Old Testament high priest even had a gold plate affixed to his turban saying, "Holiness to the Lord." If he needed a sign, he was acting something out, pointing to the true and real priest who would eventually come.

This performance took place annually on the Day of Atonement. Once a year, the high priest prepared to enter the Holy of Holies by cleansing himself with water. (Needing to physically and symbolically cleanse oneself is not a good start for one who intends to secure God's favor for the nation.) Then he would put on his special garments, testifying to his inadequacy. Next he would take two goats, placing the guilt of the people on one goat for slaughter and sending away the other, the scapegoat, to remove the sins of God's people. Finally, he would sacrifice an animal for himself and would go into the Holy of Holies with the blood. We know from other writings that bells were added to his outfit, so that people listening on the outside would know if he had been struck down.

But Jesus Christ lacked these problems. The law appointed men in their weakness as high priests, but the word of an oath (which came later than the law) appointed a Son who was made perfect forever. On the one hand, the Levitical high priest was a sinful man, offering animal sacrifices for sinful people. On the other hand, Jesus was the sinless Son of God, offering himself for the sin of all men. Because he was the sinless Son of God, he was equipped for his office as no human high priest could ever be. He was holy, so he could be our Redeemer.

"Who is the true priest?" Jesus Christ was the one to whom all the priests before him pointed, the one who was holy, blameless, and pure, the one qualified to sacrifice once for all with the offering of his own blood, able to redeem us from sin and reconcile us to God. He is our holy Redeemer. This is the great point of the book of Hebrews: whatever you have to lose in order to gain this salvation, you must count as a bargain. If you have all the world, but you do not have the holy Redeemer, you are lost. But if you have this holy Redeemer and you are kicked out of your family or are not allowed into the synagogue, or if you are fired from your job and therefore lose your house, your gain outweighs your loss. Someday we may have the opportunity in America to recognize, through persecution, what others throughout the world have learned. What a blessing it is when the people of God realize that Jesus Christ is all that they need!

When I am administering and then receiving the sacrament of the Lord's Supper, I hold the bread and cup in my hand and say, "This is all I need. I have no need of anything else." I don't want to have trials. I have a wonderful plan for my life, and in my plan, there are no trials. But God loves me more than I love myself. I want to be happy; he wants me to be holy. I want to have a good life; he wants me to display his glory in my life. And so he brings trials. I know I may have to lose everything for Jesus, but all I need is the shed blood of the Son of God. He is the true lamb; he is the high priest. If by faith I receive his provision, I have God and all the blessings of God. That's the great message of the writer of Hebrews.

In addition to being our sacrifice and our high priest, one final thing for which Jesus is perfectly fitted is our worship. The teachings of this passage are essential to our worship. Where does true worship begin? Just as there are four things to know about a sacrifice, so also there are four things to know about worship. First, true worship begins with an awareness of our need. Hebrews 7 says that Jesus meets our need, but first we need to accept and admit our need for forgiveness, our need for reconciliation with God, our need for the gift of eternal life. Without confessing that need, we will never really worship God, even though we may come to church. If we think that we are accepted by God because we are such great people, then we are greatly deceived. God will not accept us if we come that way. We come by the way made by the holy Redeemer, the perfect high priest, no matter how loathsome we may be and no matter how great we know our sin to be. Through him, we may come to God and be received and blessed.

Unless we humble ourselves before the holy God, acknowledging our need for mercy and grace and realizing that we will not be saved unless God himself saves us, we are not worshiping the true God. We are worshiping ourselves and our own religious attainments. According to Isaiah 57:15, "This is what the high and lofty One says—he who lives forever, whose name is holy: 'I live in a high and holy place, but also with him who is contrite and lowly in spirit, to revive the spirit of the lowly and to revive the heart of the contrite'" (NIV). So before going to worship, we need to realize that in Jesus Christ, God has met our need.

Our word *worship* comes from the Old English expression *worth ship*. To worship something is to acclaim it worthy. To worship, a person must realize that Jesus Christ is not just some fine moral teacher or some guru. Yet isn't that how he is viewed today in our culture? I was listening the other night on my car radio to Michael Savage, and he was talking with a Buddhist. They were talking about how all religions are the same—Jesus, Buddha, all gurus. But that's not true. Jesus is uniquely worthy. He is the Savior we need, because he did what no other could do: he offered his blood, and it was accepted by God. He is the holy priest who could deliver the sacrifice so that sinners could be reconciled. He is the only solution to our predicament, the only lamb able to bury our sin before God, the only priest able to offer that sacrifice to God. Realizing all that, we will worship.

Indeed, if you do not worship Jesus Christ, then you must not understand your need, the holiness of the true God, or the sufficiency of the saving work accomplished by Jesus. If you do not worship Jesus Christ, then you are not saved, because he alone meets your true need; he alone is fitted to your predicament before God, a sinner in the presence of the holy God. As we read the Bible, we find the redeemed in heaven worshiping the true lamb, the holy Redeemer, the one who is offered for our sin. In the book of Revelation, the apostle John opens up for us a window into heaven, where he sees a lamb that was slain sitting upon the throne, and he hears this song of heavenly joy: "Worthy are you . . . for you were slain, and by your blood you ransomed people for God from every tribe and language and people and nation, and you have made them a kingdom and priests to our God, and they shall reign on the earth" (Rev. 5:9–10). That song tells us that those who were once sinners, but now are perfected in holiness in heaven and have been made priests themselves to serve before God—even they glorify Jesus for his work. He is the lamb; he is the priest; he is our holy Redeemer who washed us by his blood. This holy high priest and the lamb of God, the redeemer Jesus Christ, is perfectly fitted for your need, and if you will admit that need—not just for a little help, but for an atoning sacrifice to take away your sins and reconcile you to God—he will take away your sin. He will open up for you the way into the presence and the blessing of the holy God, such that he will become your Father and you will be his dear child—and one day you will serve him in his presence. In the beauty of holiness, you will serve him with joy forevermore.

8

The Spirit of Holiness

MICHAEL A. G. HAYKIN

AS CHRISTIANS, we speak often of the "Holy Spirit," but far less often of the "Spirit of holiness." In order to examine rightly the third person of the blessed Trinity in these nuanced terms, we need to review some thoughts regarding the notion of holiness. After orienting ourselves thus, I want us to consider the holiness of the Spirit in relation to his person. Mostly, however, I want to look at some passages of Scripture. First we will look at Romans 1:1–4, which introduces the term "Spirit of holiness." Then we will examine other texts—one from Romans 15, two in Romans 8, and finally 1 Thessalonians 4—which speak about the Spirit of holiness and his work as our sanctifier.

A number of months ago I came across a book entitled simply *Holiness*. The author, Hannah Harrington, gives a historical look at the thinking about holiness in Jewish circles prior to and at the time of the New Testament, as well as the concept of holiness in the thinking of the Greek and Roman world. There's quite a contrast between how the Jews thought about holiness, reflecting upon their Old Testament heritage, and how the pagan Greeks and Romans thought about morality. The Jewish view serves as significant background as we come to the New Testament's description of the Holy Spirit as the Spirit of holiness. To first-century and earlier Jews, *holy* described God more closely than any other designation. His very essence is holiness. Holiness is God's innermost reality, to which all his attributes are related. In other words, for the Jews of the first century and earlier, God's holiness spoke of his transcendence, his otherness, his perfection, and his exalted power that brings people to admire and fear him. But linked to this description is the conviction that God is completely benevolent as part of his holiness, that he is utterly beneficent and wholly righteous in his exercise of justice and mercy.

Holiness is a characteristic that is uniquely innate to God. Therefore, to describe the Spirit using this term is to say something profound about his nature. Now if you go through the New Testament to search out the doctrine of the Trinity, you will not find abundant discussions of the person and the nature of the Spirit. There are clues that the Spirit is the almighty God, a member of the Godhead, not a creature—clues implying enough for later Christian thought to bring out what the New Testament is laying as a groundwork.

In the fourth century, a number of theologians were raised up by God to explicate these hints. Basil of Caesarea, Gregory of Nyssa, and Gregory of Nazianzus (as well as others whose names are not well known today) explicated what it means to describe the Spirit as holy. They drew out the conclusion that he must partake of the holiness of God, and, since holiness is innate to him, he must be God. Basil, writing in 373, says,

> We glorify the Holy Ghost together with the Father and
> the Son, from the conviction that He is not separated from

the Divine Nature; for that which is foreign by nature does not share in the same honors. . . . The creature is sanctified; it is the Spirit that sanctifies. Whether you name angels, archangels, or all the heavenly powers, they receive their sanctification through the Spirit, but the Spirit Himself has His holiness by nature, not received by favour, but essentially His; whence He has received the distinctive name of Holy.[1]

Basil draws out the implications of the phrase "Spirit of holiness"—what it means in terms of the Spirit's person: "What then is by nature holy, as the Father is by nature holy, and the Son by nature holy, we do not ourselves allow to be separated and severed from the divine and blessed Trinity."[2]

We could profitably spend time thinking about the person and nature of the Spirit, but it's also important to go further, focusing on the Spirit's work, on his making holy—and of that work there is abundant testimony in Scripture. I want to look at a few of the texts that speak about the Spirit as the giver of holiness and examine what these texts imply for our lives today.

First of all, although Romans 1:3–4 primarily speaks about the Son and the gospel that is centered on the Lord Jesus Christ, it significantly states that Christ "was descended from David according to the flesh and was declared to be the Son of God in power *according to the Spirit of holiness* by his resurrection from the dead." The Spirit is described here as the "Spirit of holiness." This is a unique phrase in the New Testament. What does it mean? Some think it's simply a synonym for *Holy Spirit*. In other words, it's simply telling us the same thing about the

1. Letter from Basil to Eupaterius and his daughter, quoted in *A Select Library of Nicene and Post-Nicene Fathers of the Christian Church*, ed. Philip Schaff and Henry Wace, vol. 8, *St. Basil: Letters and Select Works* (New York: The Christian Literature Company, 1895), 212.
2. Ibid.

Spirit's character, expressed in a different form. But it is likely telling us more than that. It is also telling us that the Spirit is the one who gives holiness. The Spirit is the one who makes real the holiness to which God has called his people. In other words, the Spirit is indispensable for the holiness that we need in our lives.

A second text that speaks to the Holy Spirit's work of holiness—this time in the hearts of Gentiles—is Romans 15:8–21. In the book of Romans, Paul is systematically laying out the gospel he preaches, because he hopes that the Roman church will be a sending church for him as he has concluded his ministry in the eastern Mediterranean and is now intending to minister in the western Mediterranean. He tells the church that he is intending to come to Rome, but not for a prolonged stay. Rather, it is for a time of mutual encouragement, as he mentions in Romans 1, but also that they might help him on his way to Spain. Here in Romans 15:8–21, Paul lays out something of his vision for his ministry:

> For I tell you that Christ became a servant to the circumcised to show God's truthfulness, in order to confirm the promises given to the patriarchs, and in order that the Gentiles might glorify God for his mercy. As it is written,
>
> > "Therefore I will praise you among the Gentiles,
> > and sing to your name."
>
> And again it is said,
>
> > "Rejoice, O Gentiles, with his people."
>
> And again,
>
> > "Praise the Lord, all you Gentiles,
> > and let all the peoples extol him."

And again Isaiah says,

> "The root of Jesse will come,
>> even he who arises to rule the Gentiles;
> in him will the Gentiles hope."

May the God of hope fill you with all joy and peace in believing, so that by the power of the Holy Spirit you may abound in hope.

I myself am satisfied about you, my brothers, that you yourselves are full of goodness, filled with all knowledge and able to instruct one another. But on some points I have written to you very boldly by way of reminder, because of the grace given me by God to be a minister of Christ Jesus to the Gentiles in the priestly service of the gospel of God, so that the offering of the Gentiles may be acceptable, sanctified by the Holy Spirit. In Christ Jesus, then, I have reason to be proud of my work for God. For I will not venture to speak of anything except what Christ has accomplished through me to bring the Gentiles to obedience—by word and deed, by the power of signs and wonders, by the power of the Spirit of God—so that from Jerusalem and all the way around to Illyricum I have fulfilled the ministry of the gospel of Christ; and thus I make it my ambition to preach the gospel, not where Christ has already been named, lest I build on someone else's foundation, but as it is written,

> "Those who have never been told of him will see,
>> and those who have never heard will understand."

This passage begins with a catena, a string of four quotations from the Old Testament that are designed to emphasize the fact that one reason that Christ came into this world was so that the Gentiles might live to the glory of God—that the Gentiles, through whom God had made none of the promises that loomed large in the minds of the Jews, might nonetheless be grafted into Israel, so that they might live to the praise and honor of God. This message was of great importance to the apostle, because he was conscious of his calling to be "a minister of Christ Jesus to the Gentiles in the priestly service of the gospel of God" (15:16).

Notice that Paul is not saying that he, as an apostle, functioned in any way, shape, or form as a priest—as a mediator between the Gentiles and God. He knew well that there was one great high priest, our Lord Jesus Christ. Rather, he is drawing imagery from the temple worship of Israel to describe his ministry. The Gentiles formerly were ritually impure. God had laid out very clearly, very distinctly, detail by detail, how God's people were to come into his presence. But the Gentiles had none of that access. They dwelt in the bondage of sin, in unrelieved spiritual darkness, far from God. But now they have become acceptable to God. How have they become acceptable? By the gospel—by their hearing of, and faith in, the gospel.

How was that faith possible? It was made possible by the Spirit. Paul describes the Gentiles as those who have been "sanctified by the Holy Spirit" (15:16). The Spirit has come into their lives, given them faith in God, and made them acceptable to God. They have been set apart; they have been sanctified. Those who were ritually impure can now come into the very presence of God with his ancient people Israel, worshiping the Lord. It is on this basis that Paul, later in this chapter, describes his readers as saints. The Spirit has sanctified them. The Spirit is holy; holiness is his by right and by nature. Now God's people can also be described as holy, not because they are holy by nature, but because the Spirit of holiness has come into their lives, given them faith, sanctified them, and set them apart for the purposes of God.

In Romans 8, Paul describes the work of the Spirit in two passages. In many respects, Romans 8 is the key chapter in Romans. There Paul talks about the work of the Spirit, but I want to focus on two passages that specifically take on the issue of sanctification: Romans 8:1–4 and Romans 8:12–14.

Romans 8:1–4 proclaims,

> There is therefore now no condemnation for those who are in Christ Jesus. For the law of the Spirit of life in Christ Jesus has set me free from the law of sin and death. For God has done what the law, weakened by the flesh, could not do: sending his own Son in the likeness of sinful flesh and for sin, he condemned sin in the flesh, in order that the just requirement of the law might be fulfilled in us, who walk not according to the flesh but according to the Spirit. (RSV)

According to this passage, Christ has come into this world to enable sinners to believe in God, to walk in ways that please him, and to obey the law. Central to that work is his death on the cross, in which he delivers sinners from the bondage of sin and sets them free. In other words, Christ's death is deliverance of the captives. But how is that deliverance made a reality in the lives of believers? It's made a reality by the Spirit. The Spirit of holiness and life has come into our lives, freeing us from the bondage of sin, enabling us now to fulfill the essence of the law. Where we were once dead in our sins, the Spirit now raises us to life and holiness. This vivifying, or "making alive," work of the Spirit is rooted in our Lord's death and resurrection.

If you want to see this vivifying and sanctifying work in action, you probably could find no better text than 1 Corinthians 6:9–11. In his autobiography, *Wounded Healer*, J. B. Phillips says that 1 Corinthians 6:9–11 is the most important passage in all of Paul's letters.[3] This elevation may be a bit exaggerated, I think, but the passage is certainly very germane to the way the Spirit comes into the lives of sinners and breaks them free from the bondage of sin:

> Do you not know that the unrighteous will not inherit the kingdom of God? Do not be deceived: neither the sexually immoral, nor idolaters, nor adulterers, nor men who practice homosexuality, nor thieves, nor the greedy, nor drunkards, nor revilers, nor swindlers will inherit the kingdom of God. And such were some of you.

This description accurately represents the people to whom Paul ministered in Corinth, as recorded in Acts 18. The eighteenth-century Baptist preacher Andrew Fuller described this city as "a sink of debauchery."[4] In fact, even the Greeks regarded the town as so immoral that "to live like a Corinthian" meant to live a godless, immoral life. In 1 Corinthians 6, Paul sketches something of the situation when he came to that city and the sort of people he found there. Deep sexual immorality, idolatry, adultery, flagrant homosexuality, thievery, greed, drunkenness—these were the habits of the people Paul encountered in Corinth. Unlike the Romans (although the Romans imitated them eventually), the Greeks believed that homosexual relations were perfectly natural. In fact, because the Greek view of women was so low and degrading, many Greeks believed that only a male could be a fit intellectual companion. No wonder Paul takes Corinth as an example of the utter rebellion and godlessness of the pagan Greek world!

---

3. See J. B. Phillips, *The Wounded Healer* (Grand Rapids: Eerdmans, 1985).
4. Andrew Fuller, *The Complete Works of the Rev. Andrew Fuller*, vol. 2 (Boston: Lincoln, Edmands, and Co., 1833), 484.

Yet Paul's message to the Corinthians does not stop there but continues: "And such were some of you. But you were washed, you were sanctified, you were justified in the name of the Lord Jesus Christ and by the Spirit of our God" (v. 11). In some respects, the most important word in this verse is the conjunction "but." It speaks of the way in which God crashed into these people's lives, tore them apart, shattered them, broke the hold of sin on their lives, and brought them to a place of faith in Christ—a place of holiness, now set apart for God's purposes and his service, to progressively make a reality in their lives what he had done for them positionally. You were justified, made right with God, washed, sanctified, and set apart in the name of our Lord Jesus Christ and by the Spirit of our God. Here we see the vivifying work of the Spirit of holiness, the way in which the Spirit brings men and women to life, breaking the death-dealing bondage of sin and cultivating in their lives the fruit of the Spirit mentioned in Galatians 5:22.

A second passage illuminating the work of the Holy Spirit is found in Romans 8:12–14.

> So then, brethren, we are debtors, not to the flesh, to live according to the flesh—for if you live according to the flesh you will die, but if by the Spirit you put to death the deeds of the body you will live. For all who are led by the Spirit of God are sons of God. (RSV)

Notice the close connection between verses 13 and 14. The leading that Paul has in mind here is not the sort often referred to today—being "led by the Spirit" to do this or that. Although that expression often has a charismatic emphasis, here the emphasis is on the leading to fight sin in one's life, a leading that has ethical and moral consequences, a leading that displays holiness lived out. If verses 1–4 talk about vivification (the Spirit coming into the life of one who is dead in his sins and making that person alive), then these verses speak about mortification (putting sin to death).

The first house that my wife and I bought was in Hamilton, Ontario. There had been only one previous owner, and he had lived there for about seventy years. Our neighbors told us how the man had planted a garden in the back and had carried stones from a nearby wood to decorate it. I believed the story, because I suspected that those stones had carried all kinds of seeds and weeds. As my wife and I tried to cultivate a garden of our own, we seemed to have every conceivable type of weed that grows in southern Ontario. If we let that garden go for a even couple of weeks, it would be entirely overrun. So I learned that there are two keys to having a weed-free garden: first, to grow what I wanted in the garden and to cultivate the new life, and, second, to dig out the weeds. Both are necessary.

So it is in the spiritual life. When the Spirit comes into our lives, he brings forth his fruit. But the other aspect, which Christians today don't often like to speak of, is the putting to death of sin. For life to exist, there needs to be a killing of all our sins. Romans 8:13 speaks of this mortification, or putting to death.

For an exposition of this truth, we can do no better than to go back three hundred years to John Owen and his discussion of *The Mortification of Sin in Believers*, originally a series of lectures to Oxford undergraduate students when he was the vice-chancellor of the university. The book has recently been reprinted by Crossway as *The Temptation of Sin*. Reading this book opened my eyes. I had spent some time in the charismatic movement, which (at least in the circles I moved in) never really dealt with the issue of sin. When I started to realize that the movement was deficient in that area (and in a couple of other areas, such as the gifts of the Spirit), I became involved with a group that emphasized what we describe as the Keswick view of holiness: just as there is a time of conversion, so you must have another crisis experience of giving all of your life to God, believing that God is done with your sin—and, from that point, it's all glory. I remember going forward as a young Christian to an altar call and thinking that I had finally dealt with sin. What a shock I soon received! Fortunately, in the providence of God, I soon after began to read the Puritans and John Owen, and I recognized a discussion of sin that was biblical, one that spoke to my experience by driving home the reality that the believer's fight against sin will not be done until he lays down his life in this world. God has set us apart to be saints; we are sanctified, and he has re-created us as new creatures. Yet even though the old things may have passed away, we are not yet in glory.

In light of this reality, Romans 8:13 states the great principle that undergirds all of Paul's ethical teaching: we ought to be what we are. "If we live by the Spirit," says Galatians 5:25, "let us also walk by the Spirit" (RSV). In other words, God has done something distinctive in our lives: he has made us saints. We've been born again; we have passed from death into life; we are now in the kingdom of his beloved Son; we are walking in the light. We need therefore to live in accordance with what we are. Don't get confused: we do not live like saints in order to become saints. Rather, we are saints and need to live in accordance with what God has already accomplished. Therefore, put sin to death in your life.

As Owen emphasizes, such mortification is ultimately the Spirit's work. He is the invincible power to overcome sin in our lives, to put it to death. But he does not do it without us. As Owens puts it,

He doth not so work our mortification in us, as not to keep it still an act of our obedience. The Holy Ghost works in us, and upon us, as we are fit to be wrought in and upon; that is, so as to preserve our own liberty and free obedience. He works upon our understandings, wills, consciences, and affections, agreeably to their own natures: he works in us and with us, not against us or without us: so that his assistance is an encouragement as to the facilitating of the work, and no occasion of neglect as to the work itself.[5]

And so the Spirit of holiness gives holiness to the people of God. He is the one who sets God's people apart. They are made saints by his coming into their lives and indwelling them. But that holiness needs to be worked out practically in everyday life. Romans 8:1–4 presents the Spirit's production of the graces, or the fruit, of the Spirit in the believer's life; Romans 8:12–14 teaches the putting to death of sin. For a holy life in the Spirit, both are needed.

Paul spoke of this work in 1 Thessalonians as well, as he wrote to those who had "turned to God from idols to serve the living and true God, and to wait for his Son from heaven, whom he raised from the dead, Jesus who delivers us from the wrath to come" (1 Thess. 1:9–10). All the sins that we see in 1 Corinthians 6 were in Thessalonica, as well—but then Paul came to that city, preaching the gospel. What did God do? According to 1 Thessalonians 1:5, "our gospel came to you not only in word, but also in power and in the Holy Spirit and with full conviction." The Spirit of God used the words of the apostle Paul to break the bondage of sin in the Thessalonians' lives and to bring them into the liberty of the gospel. But after only a few weeks, Paul

5. John Owen, *The Mortification of Sin in Believers* (repr., London: The Religious Tract Society, 1842), 26–27.

was forced to leave Thessalonica because of persecution, so he was concerned about how the church in Thessalonica was faring. He was very cognizant that these were young believers who would inevitably face pressure to revert to paganism with all of the mores and perspectives of the Greek and Roman culture. He was inescapably conscious of the sexual immorality abounding in the city. A person could not walk down a Greek or Roman street without being confronted visually with signs of immorality. The statues that we look upon today as marvelous depictions of the human form then functioned in a pornographic context. Even a seemingly innocent act—a person sharing a meal at his pagan neighbor's home—might uncover a scene of immorality.

Paul, knowing how these new believers' world would press upon them, wrote in 1 Thessalonians 4:3–8,

> For this is the will of God, your sanctification: that you abstain from sexual immorality; that each one of you know how to control his own body in holiness and honor, not in the passion of lust like the Gentiles who do not know God; that no one transgress and wrong his brother in this matter, because the Lord is an avenger in all these things, as we told you beforehand and solemnly warned you. For God has not called us for impurity, but in holiness. Therefore whoever disregards this, disregards not man but God, who gives his Holy Spirit to you.

Paul could easily have stopped at verse 3: "For this is the will of God, your sanctification," your holiness. But he was very conscious that he was called as an apostle to give explicit instructions on how to live. The average Greek or Roman of Paul's day saw nothing wrong with extramarital sexual affairs, as long as they were conducted in moderation. A fourth-century writer known as pseudo-Demosthenes shamelessly pointed to the rampant double standard for men and women when he said, "We have courtesans for pleasure, concubines for the daily tending of the body, and wives in order to beget legitimate children and have a trustworthy guardian of what is at home."[6]

However, such a lifestyle is utterly opposed to the Spirit of God. In Galatians 5:19, Paul spells out that the Spirit stands in unrelieved opposition to all such things as sexual immorality (*porneia*), impurity (*akatharsia*), and licentiousness (*aselgia*). Now, Paul was very aware that God has made us sexual beings and that sexuality has an honored place within the context of marriage—you can see that fleshed out in Ephesians 5 and 1 Corinthians 7. But "this is the will of God, your sanctification: that you abstain from sexual immorality" (1 Thess. 4:3).

As Paul further unfolds this concept of sanctification, he charges that "each one of you know how to control his own body in holiness and honor" (v. 4). The King James Version renders the text literally: "Every one of you should know how to possess his vessel in sanctification and honour." But what does Paul mean by "vessel"? There are two interpretations. One, dating back to Augustine, is that "vessel" is a euphemism for "wife." The Revised Standard Version translates it this way when it says, "Each one of you [ought to] know how to take a wife for himself in holiness and honor." In that case, Paul would be saying that believers need to avoid sexual immorality by getting married. Usually the text that's used to support this interpretation is 1 Peter 3. But in 1 Peter 3, you'll notice that the woman is called the "weaker vessel" (v. 7). In that case, the man is a vessel, too. So a better way of understanding this verse, supported by Calvin, may be to take "vessel" to mean "our bodies." In other words, Paul is talking here about believers' need to lead lives of self-control. The English Standard Version supports that understanding: "that

6. *Apollodoros "Against Neaira" [D. 59]*, trans. and ed. Konstantinos A. Kapparis (New York: Walter de Grutyer, 1999), 161.

each one of you [ought to] know how to control his own body in holiness and honor." Sanctification involves self-control in sexual matters, a refusal to use one's body to satisfy one's sexual thirst, because now our bodies are made for glory.

On the Internet a few weeks ago, I saw an interview of Joel Osteen on *Larry King Live*—a fascinating interview from a number of perspectives. During the interview, Larry King asked Osteen if he believes in hell. He does. But Osteen went on to talk about his trust in the life to come and said, "I believe we're all going to live on, that we're a spirit. This body—I like to think of it as just like my coat. There's something on the inside of me that's making this thing move. . . . The real me is on the inside."[7] I thought, "What I'm hearing is second-century Gnosticism." The view that our bodies will one day be trash was and is heresy, because for the apostle Paul and for all New Testament believers, the body was essential to who you are. If we talk about "having" a body, that's actually very Greek. In Hebrew thinking, we *are* bodies. That is why Paul insists that our bodies have been joined to the Lord and that the Spirit of the Lord Jesus Christ has come to indwell this body. This body is made for glory; one day, this body will be raised from the dead. Therefore, how dare I indulge this body in sexual immorality?

Paul grounds these affirmations about the need to pursue holiness with three reasons. First of all, the Lord is an avenger in all these things. This view is affirmed in Hebrews 13:4: "Let marriage be held in honor among all, and let the marriage bed be undefiled, for God will judge the sexually immoral and adulterous." We serve a holy God, and it is an awesome thing to fall into his hands as sinners.

7. Joel and Victoria Osteen, interview by Larry King, *Larry King Live*, CNN, October 16, 2007, transcript available online at http://transcripts.cnn.com/TRANSCRIPTS/0710/16/lkl.01.html.

Secondly, God calls believers to turn away from all impurity, to pursue holiness. In this way, we need to be more like the early Methodists. We who love Reformed theology sometimes look askance at John Wesley and the Methodist tradition, but there's much to admire in their passion for preaching the gospel. As principal of Toronto Baptist Seminary, I have had a picture of John Wesley put up at the entrance to the seminary building. Some Reformed brothers and sisters wonder, "What is that guy doing there?" But I reply, "Would that Reformed preachers today had his passion for the salvation of sinners!" Equally, would that Reformed men and women had his passion for holiness! Wesley used to talk about Methodists' need to be "on the stretch," reaching out for holiness. Although there are areas where I radically disagree with Wesley's teaching, on the topic of the pursuit of holiness, he's on point.

Thirdly, Paul says that our sanctification concerns not man, but God. In other words, if you don't listen to these words, you're not rejecting the words of a first-century rabbi who became a believer in Jesus. You're rejecting—and this has all kinds of implications for the canon—the words of the living God. There is a consciousness here that Paul's words are inspired Scripture.

Paul could have easily stopped there. God is a holy God; he will judge sin. God calls believers to a life of holiness. Now, he does not call us to perfection in this life; otherwise, we would not have Romans 8:12–14. So do not go away discouraged. Rather, make the same commitment that eighteenth-century minister Jonathan Edwards made when he wrote his resolutions in his early twenties. To paraphrase his language, he resolved never to give up fighting sin, despite failing.

In the same way, we wrestle with sin; we spend our whole life fighting sin. But Paul goes on to emphasize that this same holy God who will judge sin gives us his Spirit. The phraseology in the Greek version of 1 Thessalonians 4:8 is very important: "Who gives his Spirit, the Holy One, to you." He doesn't simply say "the Holy Spirit." He emphasizes the word *holy* for two reasons. First of all, somebody might ask, "How do I know that God is calling me to a holy life?" "Well," Paul says, "who is the one who brought you to faith in the Lord Jesus Christ? Who is the one who convinced you that the words I was preaching were the words of the living God? None other than the Spirit of God. The Holy Spirit now indwells you—and he never, ever comes without his holy, moral character."

Much discussion has taken place over the past years with the charismatic movement, the Third Wave, and the Throne of Blessing about the work of the Spirit. Often lost in that discussion is the holiness that the Spirit brings into the lives of believers. He never, ever comes without his character. Therefore, we must always remember that the God who speaks to us is the God who gives his Holy Spirit to us.

In emphasizing that God gives his Spirit, Paul's words hark back to Ezekiel 36:27 and 37:14. There God promises a great day of the new covenant. In the new covenant, the Spirit will be given to enable law-keeping to be a reality. The Spirit will come in and transform lives. Second Corinthians 3:18 also talks about the transforming work of the Spirit, a fulfillment of those passages in Ezekiel. God will put his Spirit within his people to enable them to keep the law.

In light of Paul's teaching, I'd like to offer some words of application. The great challenge we have today in embracing this teaching of the holiness of the triune God and the Spirit's sanctifying work is that they go hand-in-hand with the idea of human depravity. In the presence of a holy God, we see ourselves for what we are—filthy, leprous, stained, stinking. We are sinners.

We need a holy Redeemer. These are not easy words for an early twenty-first century person, even a believer. We don't live in an environment that encourages this sort of thought. Nevertheless, we desperately need the Spirit of God in our lives. Without him, all is vain in the work of sanctification and holiness.

It's not new that we live in a world in which men and women don't see themselves as sinners. We might say that this has always been the case, and we can find plenty of evidence of this mind-set in the past. In the eighteenth century, one of the aristocratic women of the day, a friend of Selina Hastings, Countess of Huntingdon, commented on George Whitfield: "I love Whitfield's preaching, so absorbing, so ravishing his thoughts, but when he goes on and talks about us as sinners and compares us to the common people, oh, it just is too much to be borne."

But I think our day is even more difficult. Listen to two men writing about our day. The first is Dominique Clift, who wrote *The Secret Kingdom* about what it means to be a Canadian. Toward the end of the book, he has three pages on the religious scene in Canada. Here he writes,

> The most significant break going on today in Canadian society with earlier religious attitudes, the one with the most far-reaching psychological consequences because of its effect on the way people see themselves, is the elimination of feelings of guilt and of unworthiness as the foundations of religious life. This development coincides with the appearance of more permissive social standards, particularly in sexual matters. . . . Somehow, religion has moved beyond ethics: what has become uppermost today is the religious experience itself.[8]

8. Dominique Clift, *The Secret Kingdom: Interpretations of the Canadian Character* (Toronto: McClelland & Stewart, 1989), 205–6.

Clift wrote this in 1989 as a description of Canada, but it is very much what the whole Western scene is currently about.

J. I. Packer describes the same phenomena: "This twentieth century has indulged unwarrantably great thoughts of humanity and scandalously small thoughts of God."[9] He predicts that our day will be known as the "age of the God-shrinkers." He says,

> Belief in God's sovereignty and omniscience, the majesty of His moral law and the terror of His judgments, the retributive consequences of the life we live here and the endlessness of the eternity in which we will experience them, along with belief in the intrinsic tri-unity of God and the divinity and personal return of Jesus Christ, is nowadays so eroded as to be hardly discernible. For many in our day, God is no more than a smudge.[10]

How do we respond to these analyses? We need to think biblically. We need to immerse ourselves again and again in biblical perspectives about God. We need to view the world through the Scriptures. We need to inhabit the Holy Word so that it becomes the medium through which we see all things. We need to radically reorient ourselves again and again to the biblical perspective: this is God's world; he is a holy God; he has made heaven and earth; he will one day come and judge all men and women by his dear Son, our Lord Jesus Christ. We need to come back again and again to these bedrock biblical truths. But we also need to take great comfort in the fact that the Spirit of God will build the church of the Lord Jesus Christ. He will prevail against the gates of hell. And even our modern sensibilities and our own sins are no barrier to his invincible power.

9. J. I. Packer, *Rediscovering Holiness: Know the Fullness of Life with God* (Ann Arbor, MI: Servant Publications, 1992; repr., Grand Rapids: Baker, 2009), 54.
10. Ibid.

I want to finish with a case study of a woman named Mary Stewart, drawn from a booklet published by InterVarsity called *Sexual Freedom*. This woman came to know Christ in that turbulent era of the late 1960s and early 1970s. She found that she had some radical choices to make in her life.

> I was a very liberated young woman at the time. I had had a rich sexual fantasy life ever since I could remember. I'd learned to masturbate efficiently at a very young age. I'd almost lost count of the number of men I'd slept with in a serially monogamous fashion. I'd taken advantage of the spirit of the woman's movement (in which I was quite active) to begin exploring my own bisexuality. I'd no intention of giving any of that up when I accepted Christ. I thought it was the spirit of the law, not the letter, that mattered—that love was the overriding principle. I could witness in bed as easily as anywhere else. But to my astonishment, I found all that changes—not quickly, not always all at once. There was a process of God working on me, one item at a time over many months, like God patiently peeling one layer after another off an onion.[11]

She goes on to talk about how God began to enable her to walk in his blessed statutes and to walk according to his laws. She quotes Ezekiel 36:27. She found herself, she says, progressively liberated and strengthened. She even says, "I would wake up in the morning by myself in bed and find deep satisfying freedom in that." Furthermore, she testifies, "I found I wanted God's spirit more than I wanted transient, physical titillation."

Because of this freedom—from sin, to holiness—we bless the Spirit of God, who has come into this world, the gift of the

11. V. Mary Stewart, *Sexual Freedom* (Downers Grove, IL: InterVarsity Press, 1974).

Lord Jesus Christ to accomplish the Son's purposes begun on the cross. He will build his church. Despite all our modern sensibilities, all of the elect will be gathered in, and the Spirit will do that great work. God's work will be done by God's Spirit—his sweet grace ultimately, thankfully, blessedly irresistible.

9

Know the Truth

R. ALBERT MOHLER

IN LONDON IN 2009, Richard Dawkins decided to go into the advertising business. Dawkins is perhaps the best-known atheist in the world right now because of his ardent advocacy of a very hard-line form of atheism. He presents his atheistic claims in a starkly straightforward and surgical manner in both writings and public appearances. He considers belief in God to be not only epistemologically unsustainable but also socially and culturally dangerous. In 2008, he gave £5,500 to support the purchase of advertising space on London buses to encourage Londoners to join atheism. But issues soon arose with the wording of the signs: "There's probably no God. Now stop worrying and enjoy your life."[1] The controversy lay in the word *probably*. In terms of public relations, the signs may have had the opposite effect of what was intended. Paul Woolley, former director of the Christian think tank Theos, even donated money to support

1. See "Atheist Bus Campaign," British Humanist Association, accessed February 15, 2016, https://humanism.org.uk/about/atheist-bus-campaign.

the campaign's effect of causing people to think about "the most important question we will ever face in our lives."[2] Responding to these advertisements, an awful lot of people in Britain have said, "*Probably?* We're basing our lives on *absolutely*. There's absolutely no God." As a result of the campaign, blogs went wild in Britain, as have many commentators who see Richard Dawkins as an atheist with failure of nerve. After all, there are people in Britain who are beginning to wonder if there actually might be a God, since the nation's most ardent atheist thinks it's just *probable* that he doesn't exist. Dawkins responded that he would have preferred the language "There is almost certainly no God," but the impossibility of proving that God definitely does not exist threatened to raise truth-in-advertising issues with the British Advertising Standards Authority.[3] At any rate, the campaign hoped to send a subversive message. But what it really ended up subverting was atheism.

Last night I took the opportunity to set up in a more academic structure several of the modern challenges to truth. After all, we are responsible to be aware of the fact that when we use the word *truth*, many people around us consider it not only to be a contested category, but also to be something very different from what Christians mean and clearly claim when they use the word. We are living among some who, like William James, believe that ideas are true if they accomplish what is needed. There are also those who believe that "truth people," people who make claims to truth, are inherently dangerous. Of course, they set that concern in the context of a truth claim that would be just

2. "Religious Think Tank Welcomes Launch of Atheist Buses," Theos, January 6, 2009, http://www.theosthinktank.co.uk/comment/2009/01/06/religious-think-tank-welcomes-launch-of-atheist-buses.

3. Ariane Sherine, "'Probably' the Best Atheist Bus Campaign Ever," *The Guardian*, October 23, 2008, http://www.theguardian.com/commentisfree/2008/oct/23/atheist-bus-campaign-ariane-sherine.

as dangerous if it were understood. They actually do not mean all claims to truth but, in particular, theistic claims to truth, because that truth makes a claim upon every single human life.

Modern epistemology suggests that we are still stuck in Plato's cave and that the best we can do is to see and talk about, and to seek to derive meaning from, shadows projected on the wall. Fundamentally, that is true about knowledge. There is a sense in which the Christian must be the first to say, "Yes, that's exactly right—but for the gift of divine revelation." Mankind is not just confused; we are blind. According to biblical theology, our epistemological state is much worse than the most suspicious teachers of epistemology could ever imagine, because we are cursed by the intellectual ravages of sin. This perspective helps us when we think about Reformed epistemology: do remember that it is humble. Its humility does not come from claiming that we do not know or cannot know; we acknowledge that we know only in part, but the part that we do know, we know. The humility here is in understanding that the church is not an elitist Mensa or gnostic society, but a community of the blind who have been given sight. We are not here because we devised a brilliant laboratory experiment, the result of which was credible evidence for belief in God. We are not here because we followed some kind of intellectual quest that led us in terms of our own self-sufficiency and intellectual capability to believe in God. We are merely the blind who have been given sight.

There is great awkwardness and often a sense of embarrassment in this understanding when it comes to matters of truth in this modern or postmodern or post-postmodern world. Whenever truth claims are asserted, there's a wink on the part of some and a grimace on the part of others. In 2 Timothy 1, Paul speaks of the Christian faith in terms of its truthfulness. In overlapping ways, it is both personal and propositional, leading to constant humility but also to confidence. The apostle Paul knows whom he has believed. He's absolutely confident of the claims upon which he has staked his life. He believes that they are true, and he recites them in terms of propositional claims—but they are, after all, also personal, related to the one whom he met on the road to Damascus, whose servant he now is.

Yes, there is great awkwardness, but we must recognize a lot of awkwardness on the part of some who should not be awkward. Too many Christian preachers are awkward when it comes to truth. Entire movements within the Christian church are increasingly awkward in this regard. There is an entire movement known as "humble theology." Those two words seem gloriously put together, except that the movement sees humility as making claims only in the most tentative sense or only in a communitarian setting. This cultural conversation is where we now find ourselves, a conversation in which some people say, "This is *our* truth; this is *our* communal meaning; this is *our* cultural-linguistic system; this is *our* confessional heritage." They seek to avoid the embarrassment of saying, "I believe the Bible's claims to be true in space, time, and history. I believe these propositional claims to be necessary but not sufficient in themselves. My religion is not just a cognitive apprehension of these propositional claims, but rather saving faith. It is far beyond, but it is not independent of, the facts."

In John 14:6, Jesus makes one of his boldest propositional claims: "I am the way, and the truth, and the life. No one comes to the Father except through me." This statement was the impetus for a conversation I once had with a pastor in the Emerging Church movement. In the midst of a conversation about truth, he defensively predicted, "You're going to throw John 14:6 at me!"

I replied, "That sounds like a self-inflicted wound. You beat me to it. You just took the gun out of my hand, pointed it at yourself, and pulled the trigger."

"Well, the problem I have with John 14:6 is that we don't know to whom Jesus is specifically referring."

"Well, I'll play along, so help me."

"Well, when you talk about Jesus being 'the way, the truth, and the life,' so that 'no man comes to the Father but by me,' it's perfectly legitimate to ask whether the *no one* there refers to all humanity or to those to whom Jesus was then speaking."

My response was blunt: "Let me ask you an honest question. If all Jesus meant was that he was true to the people to whom he was then speaking, why do you care?" I won't continue that conversation, because it went more or less nowhere. There was an absolute refusal on the part of my conversation partner to come to terms with what even he admitted had to be the claim the text is making upon the church. A humility built on denial of the truth is a wrong kind of humility.

I love what author Josh Harris and others are doing when they redefine the movement of "humble orthodoxy" as having both a humble spirit and a glad apprehension of the claims of and witness to orthodox Christianity. If *humility* refers to our attitude, then biblical believers should be there. If we show up with anything less than that kind of humility, sin is upon us, because we are the blind who have been given sight, not the investigators who have found the prize. But the wrong kind of humility seems to be so very close at hand.

This temptation to adopt a perverted humility is a serious issue for Christians when we consider the frequency of Christ's bold propositional claims. When Christ refers to himself as "the way, and the truth, and the life," it is merely the culmination of a series of striking "I am" statements in the gospel of John. Every one of the "I am" statements reveals Christ's deity, disclosing his divine identity and, in this case, supremely and definitively presenting himself as the way, and the truth, and the life. These statements are indeed personal calls to truth; Christ is calling for those who hear his words to believe in him. But he is also making very clear statements in the propositional sense concerning who he is. The claim these days is that truth must be either personal or propositional, but in Christ the personal and the propositional, as well as truth far beyond those categories, are melted together in an infinite harmony.

However, I'd like for us to focus not on John 14 but on John 6. When I think of a passage in John in which all these truths come together in short, compact verses, my mind immediately goes to John 6:60–69:

> When many of his disciples heard it, they said, "This is a hard saying; who can listen to it?" But Jesus, knowing in himself that his disciples were grumbling about this, said to them, "Do you take offense at this? Then what if you were to see the Son of Man ascending to where he was before? It is the Spirit who gives life; the flesh is no help at all. The words that I have spoken to you are spirit and life. But there are some of you who do not believe." (For Jesus knew from the beginning who those were who did not believe, and who it was who would betray him.) And he said, "This is why I told you that no one can come to me unless it is granted him by the Father."
>
> After this many of his disciples turned back and no longer walked with him. So Jesus said to the Twelve, "Do you want to go away as well?" Simon Peter answered him, "Lord, to whom shall we go? You have the words of eternal life, and we have believed, and have come to know, that you are the Holy One of God."

Thanks be to God for his Word! In these short verses, we have a seminar of Jesus with his disciples—and it is an awkward seminar. What occasioned this awkwardness? Earlier in John 6, Christ reveals himself as the Bread of Life. The crowd has come to find him on the day after the feeding of the five thousand and his walking on the water. When they find Jesus on the other side of the sea, they ask him, "Rabbi, when did you come here?" (v. 25). Jesus answers them, "Truly, truly, I say to you, you are seeking me, not because you saw signs, but because you ate your fill of the loaves" (v. 26). In other words, he calls them out: "I know why you're here, and it's not for a sermon. You're not here because you have believed in me. You are here because you want to see the spectacle again and you want to be filled." In John 6:27, he continues to admonish them: "Do not work for the food that perishes, but for the food that endures to eternal life"—at which point the metaphor becomes unmistakably clear—"which the Son of Man will give to you. For on him God the Father has set his seal." Then they ask, "What must we do, to be doing the works of God?" (v. 28). What a dangerous question! Jesus answers, "This is the work of God, that you believe in him whom he has sent" (v. 29).

Jesus reveals here the very purpose for which he came: that sinners would believe in him. This is the work of God that we are called to do. If you want to know what God has commanded you to do, it comes down to a very short imperative: believe. Of course, this isn't belief without an object. We are not justified by faith in faith. We are justified by faith in Christ, for "Jesus said to them, 'I am the bread of life; whoever comes to me shall not hunger, and whoever believes in me shall never thirst'" (v. 35). Previously, John 4 revealed Christ as the everlasting water that eternally sustains life. Here we learn of him as the bread of life, as well.

The command of God was that sinners believe, but in reality most do not believe. Here we have an epistemological problem.

Belief is a central issue. We come back to it again and again. According to John 6, a refusal to deal directly with Christ's truth claim and to recognize the imperative of belief is a refusal to come to terms with the way Jesus describes himself, his ministry, God's command, and the gospel. Jesus repeatedly circles around those who have come to confront him, bringing up again and again their unbelief. They are the willing blind who refuse to see: "I said to you that you have seen me and yet do not believe" (v. 36). He makes clear that they choose between belief and unbelief.

In the midst of this challenge, Jesus states a universal positive principle of the atonement: "All that the Father gives me will come to me, and whoever comes to me I will never cast out" (v. 37). From this reality comes my absolute confidence in preaching the Word of God. On the basis of the authority of the Lord Jesus Christ himself, I know that all whom the Father calls will come. Otherwise, I don't know what I would do—but it certainly wouldn't be simple biblical preaching. It would have to be something a bit flashier than that, something with a little more psychological technique, something with a more substantial hook. If I didn't have the confidence that all whom the Father gives to the Son will come to him, I could not preach the Word.

On the other hand, John 6:44 states the universal negative principle of the atonement: "No one can come to me unless the Father who sent me draws him. And I will raise him up on the last day." Now, here is substantial ground for epistemological humility. We were drawn. We have come to know that Jesus is the Christ and have received him and believed that he is the truth only because we were drawn. Not only were we given sight when blind, but we were captured, taken, pulled in. This is effectual calling—and thank God! In our sinfulness, we would have rejected the truth as unworthy of belief.

Jesus supplies the object of that belief in John 6:47–48: "Truly, truly, I say to you, whoever believes has eternal life. I am the bread of life." Again, we are saved not by belief in belief, nor by faith in faith; this faith has an object. Jesus makes clear that he himself is the object:

> I am the bread of life. Your fathers ate the manna in the wilderness, and they died. This is the bread that comes down from heaven, so that one may eat of it and not die. I am the living bread that came down from heaven. If anyone eats of this bread, he will live forever. And the bread that I will give for the life of the world is my flesh. (vv. 48–51)

What a clear teaching of Christ's substitutionary work on the cross!

After this clear but bold teaching, the Jews disputed among themselves, saying, "How can this man give us his flesh to eat?" (v. 52). So Jesus said to them, "Truly, truly, I say to you, unless you eat the flesh of the Son of Man and drink his blood, you have no life in you" (v. 53). Jesus doesn't back up here. He doesn't take a new tack or trim his sails; there is no artificial humility. He continues along the same line:

> For my flesh is true food, and my blood is true drink. Whoever feeds on my flesh and drinks my blood abides in me, and I in him. As the living Father sent me, and I live because of the Father, so whoever feeds on me, he also will live because of me. This is the bread that came down from heaven. (vv. 55–58)

This "bread from heaven" is not manna in the morning, but the incarnation of the Christ.

Jesus said these things in the synagogue as he taught. When many of his disciples heard it, they said, "This is a hard saying;

who can listen to it?" (v. 60). Oh no! This resistance is where we live. I spend a lot of time in bookstores, and in almost every bookstore I visit, John 6 comes very much to mind. "This is a hard saying!" That's what our culture is saying. Just scanning the book titles, you can hear it. If we are honest, we have to admit that, had we been there, we would probably have done no better than the half-hearted disciples and the hard-hearted Jews.

And the disciples do look bad. To me, one of the central arguments in favor of the authenticity of the New Testament is how badly the disciples come off. This gospel was not written by a public relations agency for the disciples after the beginning of the church in the book of Acts. These stories are brutal reality. Many of his disciples said, "This is a hard saying!" and Jesus responded, "I am the bread of life. Here's the deal: you believe in me, you live; you reject this, you die. You have no life in you whatsoever. And it is the Father's command that you believe. Life and death come down to this. And just in case you just missed the point, if you do not eat my flesh and drink my blood, there is no life in you." Talk about a public relations disaster! Some who had identified with Jesus, who had been walking with him in the larger group, heard those words as overly harsh, as claiming too much. Where is the epistemological humility, Jesus?

And Jesus walks right into it: "Jesus, knowing in himself that his disciples were grumbling about this, said to them, 'Do you take offense at this?'" (v. 61). The drama in John 6 is absolutely incredible. Imagine Jesus turning to those who were his own disciples and saying, "Have you got a problem with this?" I want to say with humility that this text has been incredibly powerful in my own life. There have been moments when I've found myself addressed by this question: "You got a problem with this?" Every time a preacher gets up to preach, he should hear that question: "You got a problem with this? If so, don't get up and preach. How in the world do you share the gospel if you've got a problem with this?"

However, if you listen to conversation in the church or to what is presented as Christian conversation in the academic world or in many different movements in the church, you will hear, "Yes, we've got a problem with this! There's got to be a different way to put it!" If Richard Dawkins had had his way with public relations, he wouldn't have used the word *probably*. If the early church had had their way with public relations, they would have found a better way to frame the gospel. But this is the Word of God; this is what Jesus said.

When Jesus asked, "Do you take offense at this?" he already knew that they were grumbling in their hearts. There is something horribly offensive to the unregenerate mind about Jesus' claim. Our effete, twenty-first–century mind considers this crude, substitutionary eating and drinking of flesh and blood to be grotesque. I recently read a biblical commentator who said that we have to admit a natural disgust at this presentation. I know what he meant, and I hate what he meant, but what he said is absolutely true: the natural man hates Jesus' claim. The natural response is, "I don't want it; I don't like it; I don't believe it." And some people identified as disciples of Jesus evidently felt the same way.

However, Jesus kept pushing the envelope: "Are you offended by this? If so, just wait for the ascension. What if you were to see the Son of Man ascending to where he was before?" Then he offers a very important principle: "It is the Spirit who gives life; the flesh is no help at all" (v. 63). That principle certainly has to do with salvation, summarizing the entirety of our understanding of the need of the sinner. But it also has everything to do with epistemology. It's the Spirit who gives life. We are not gnostics. The apostle Paul says there is a mystery, but it is a mystery that has been unveiled. The problem is not that the truth is not clear; the problem is that sinful eyes cannot see it. We have become believers in the Lord Jesus Christ because what once was offensive now becomes sweet. However, this change doesn't happen because we are in any way intellectually more capable than those who remain disgusted by it. "The Spirit gives life; the flesh profits nothing. The words that I have spoken to you," Jesus says, "are spirit and life"—as set over against the flesh and all efforts of a natural theology. Spirit and life provide rescue from Plato's cave and from our epistemological dilemma. We didn't crawl out of the cave; we were rescued. Again, look at how Jesus juxtaposes belief and unbelief, adding, "There are some of you who do not believe" (v. 64).

In one conversation with a young pastor, I asked him, "Can you preach this text?"

He said, "Oh, certainly."

I said, "I'd love to hear it. Tell me when you're going to preach on this text, and I'll buy a plane ticket to hear it. Just try out on me what you would say."

"These are the words we have come to know and cherish; this is the church's language."

"I'm not flying out for that," I said. "That's a very short sermon."

But the pastor's sermon would have worked well by public relations standards. Why would anyone walk away, if it's only a matter of church language? If this is merely our story, our cultural-linguistic system, our confession—if this is just who we are and what is meaningful to us—who needs to grumble about that? If this is where we happen to find the connection between the earthly and the power of the divine, no one would object, except perhaps on the basis of aesthetic taste.

Tribalism is not a problem in today's intellectual world. Tribalism *is* the modern culture. You are allowed to have your own private little truth system, your own private language, your own private confession. However, the price of your being allowed to do this is that you may not claim that anyone else should accept your belief as true. By believing, in today's society, you are not making a universal, objective, totalitarian, hegemonic, patriarchal, and oppressive truth claim; you are simply saying in humility, "This is who we are. This is our little band, and this is our story."

Yet for Christians one key issue remains: is there anything in that sort of preaching that would lead anyone to walk away? If not, then we have to consider how much like Christ's message ours really is. Jesus here makes very clear that the truth is personal; he is the person who is the truth. But it's also propositional. Jesus' disciples didn't walk away because they didn't like him; they walked away because they couldn't take what Jesus claimed about himself. His were propositional claims. They were truth claims, and they were understood to be truth claims.

Several years ago, a good friend set me up for a public debate in a very large auditorium in Washington, D.C. We were debating basic issues related to Christian truth—not a debate between an atheist and a believer, but rather between a conservative evangelical and a more liberal Protestant. I agreed to do the debate because at that particular moment it appeared that defining the issues might be helpful to a denominational body trying to make some basic decisions. As it turned out, the evangelicals evidently had not been told about the debate, but the other side had come in great numbers. I discovered immediately that that was one of the most liberating experiences I've ever had. I might not have gotten out alive, but at least I was going to have a glorious opportunity to say what I had come to say.

I also discovered a personal limit I had not known before. I toed the edge of self-control, and I fell over it. At that debate, a NASA scientist working in Washington said to me, "I want none of your propositional theology. I want none of these truth claims, and I insist that Christianity has nothing to do with them except by the imposition of fundamentalists and conservative evangelicals. We have emerged out of a medieval mind-set and are now in an epistemological position in which you are an embarrassment to the church. All I want is Jesus Christ; I want no theology." That's when I dove. I said, "Sir, you are not a Christian. Do you think there was a mailbox in Judah that said 'Christ, Jesus'? Do you think *Christ* is a surname? You said you want to have Jesus Christ. I want you to have Jesus Christ. But when you say "Jesus Christ," you are saying that Jesus is the Messiah, the Anointed One. You are making a theological claim. That is not a first and last name. That is a confession of faith. Welcome to theology! You are a theologian. You either believe it, or you do not."

By the grace of God, I recovered and clambered back up the cliff. Sometimes, you hear yourself saying things you never planned to say. But to me, that was a John 6 moment. I realized, "Here are people who say 'Jesus Christ' and think they are not even making a claim. They think, in their epistemological humility, that they are merely referring to a person." But you know there is a sweet irony in this, isn't there? All the people who keep referring to him by this name actually don't realize that they are making a statement of faith.

So much of what's going on in contemporary theology reflects its admittedly sophisticated attempt to overcome the facts. If you live and work and breathe in an academic setting, these realities are around you all the time. But it is not just in the academic setting. This view of truth has filtered down to the level of popular culture. The average fourteen-year-old in middle school or high school is being confronted with this kind of intellectual subversion in the post- and post-postmodern view of truth.

The other day I was talking to a fifteen-year-old enrolled in a prestigious prep school. He told me about an essay assignment on what we would call "worldview." He was a well-catechized young man, so his essay set out more or less the entirety of the Christian faith. Now, his teacher is a Buddhist, and the class is overwhelmingly made up of skeptics. But when he read his paper, no one was offended. He had worked up all his answers to potential questions, but there was no offense. Do you know why there was no offense? They heard it as his story. They said, "This is you. This helps us to understand you." Such is the humble epistemological smile of the culture that says, "We know you better now."

Notice that those who were grumbling about Jesus didn't say, "Oh, Jesus, we understand you so much better now. We understand your worldview. We understand what makes you tick. We know you so much better now." No, they said, "We'll have nothing to do with this." Jesus didn't allow elasticity of understanding. He didn't leave it vague. He went directly to, "If you will not eat my flesh or drink my blood, then there is no life in you." Then, when some of his disciples grumbled, he said, "You got a problem with this? Well, you just wait."

Now we are told already that at this moment of crisis, some of the grumblers walked with him no more. Some who claimed to be his disciples left. We certainly have seen that response throughout the history of the church, and it arose very quickly in the early church. Even then, people took issue with Christ's propositional claims. They also already manifested the problem with humble theology: it's humble in the wrong ways.

However, some in the early church did get it right. In the book of Acts, I find a very humble church. As a matter of fact, their social, economic, and political vulnerabilities required humility. But that humility did not keep Peter and John from speaking to the Sanhedrin with a very straightforward, propositional, narrative, and personal presentation of the gospel of Jesus Christ. On the day of Pentecost, humility didn't prevent Peter from announcing that "the man you killed was none other than the Christ" (see Acts 4). It didn't keep the apostles from declaring the truth in a clear, profound, and powerful way—and it didn't keep the world from responding with offense.

The young pastor with whom I spoke tried hard to avoid this response. He told me, with absolute conviction in his position, "One of my goals is to be able to preach such that persons are seduced into faith in Christ." I said, "You know, there's a sense in which that sounds so attractive to me. The problem I have with that approach is what the apostle Paul said his ministry looked like: 'I got let down in a basket from a window in Damascus; I've been flogged; I've been stoned; I've been shipwrecked.' I just can't picture the apostle Paul in the colloquium of ministry saying, 'Here's what I discovered. You seduce people into the gospel.'"

That approach to ministry is wrong at so many levels. It's wrong in its understanding of our role in others' salvation. There's an irresistible call, but it's not the effectual call of the postmodern preacher. It's the effectual call of the Holy Spirit. It's not something we can manipulate. It's not something we can often even see. When Jesus spoke of the Spirit to Nicodemus, he said, "The wind blows where it wishes" (John 3:8), and you see its effects after it blows. We see the result of it, but we do not see the operations.

An even more pressing and urgent issue for us is not just what Jesus said that caused the larger group to grumble; it's

146

what Jesus then said when he turned to the Twelve: "This is why I told you that no one can come to me unless it is granted him by the Father" (John 6:65). We believers are not here because we brought ourselves here intellectually or willfully. We are here because we were drawn; we are here because the Father gave us to the Son. "No one can come to me unless it is granted him by the Father"—that's a hard saying. It's a hard saying about a hard saying. Jesus sounds as if he is going to explain why the first saying is so hard, but the response is another hard saying itself.

How many people in our churches believe that no one can come to Christ unless it is granted to him or her by the Father? Try speaking those words—just those words—in a large evangelical assembly and see what happens. If this prerequisite for belief is true, then much of what is considered evangelism isn't, and much of what is considered ministerial technique is a lie. We either hate this saying or find our confidence in it. There is really no middle ground. By God's grace, we must find our confidence in this. That's our confidence in proclaiming the gospel and teaching the Word. We open the Scripture and preach it, declare Christ and present his claims, just because God himself uses these words in order to call men and women to Christ. And he does call; he does give; he does grant.

John 6:66 summarizes the result of preaching the truth: "After this many of his disciples turned back and no longer walked with him." They had reached a breaking point. Here we have a crisis in the ministry of Jesus. The band of disciples was getting smaller precisely over the question of truth and Jesus' insistence on pressing the issue of truth. Had Jesus spoken these things only to his disciples, it might have led to a very different response on the part of this larger band who grumbled. But Jesus made this propositional claim in public, and he said it precisely to those who were the enemies of the gospel. He said it in such a public way that it caused embarrassment.

Is *embarrassment* not the word that best fits much contemporary Christianity or self-styled Christianity? You know, we have come to expect this embarrassment, this cognitive diminution of the faith, this doctrinal disarmament among those who are liberals. We come to expect that. That's how they got there. That was their manifesto. It's important for us to recognize that and be reminded of that. It's significant that we go back to specific points in history, specific controversies and decisions made or unmade, specific trajectories in denominations or churches. We ought to track that, to know those stories.

But as close as that narrative is to us as a matter of exhortation, it isn't enough. We need to recognize that the same kind of embarrassment is present among many who would insist that they are not liberals and that they are not seeking a doctrinal reformulation of the faith. They simply want to reconstitute and reframe the way that we understand the faith and communicate it. Many of their criticisms of contemporary evangelicalism are valid. That's the hard part. The problem is that their answer to these issues is a theological humility that doesn't fit Jesus. In fact, it is a humility that Jesus directly condemned to the extent that many of those who walked with him walked with him no more.

There are certain places and times and events in history that I'm not sure I could have withstood personally. Even looking back, I've been through a lot over fifty years that I do not want to go through again. But I'm glad I was not on the scene of John 6 when Jesus asked the Twelve, "Do you want to go away? The exit signs are at the back. Your bus will not wait. It's a reverse invitation. That way is the way out." I'm certainly glad that I was never with Jesus in the region of Caesarea Philippi and faced with the question, "Who do people say that the Son of Man is?" (Matt. 16:13). Now that would have been tough. And I'm certainly glad I wasn't there when Jesus asked, "But who do you say that I am?" (v. 15). I feel much more confident addressing that question now that we have the data, the confession of the Word of God, the authoritative answer to the question.

But Peter knew the answer to the question: "You are the Christ, the Son of the living God" (v. 16). And then Jesus said, "How brilliant are you, Peter, for you have crawled painstakingly out of Plato's cave. You have transcended your epistemological crisis; you have matured into a knower. You have discovered the secret; your laboratory has produced the answer; your theorem is now demonstrated publicly."

No. Rather, Jesus said, "Blessed are you, Simon Bar-Jonah! For flesh and blood has not revealed this to you, but my Father who is in heaven" (v. 17). In our humility, we've got to admit that our epistemological problem is not only as bad as the modern hermeneuts of suspicion would suggest. The prophets of hermeneutical suspicion are not only right; they are a lot more right than they know.

But Peter was right in more than one way. When Jesus asked the Twelve, "Do you want to go away as well?" Peter answered him, "Lord, to whom shall we go?" (John 6:68). Now there is epistemological humility in its essence: "Okay, Lord, in all honesty, we have to admit we don't have options here. We are standing here, not because we are smarter than those who left, more spiritually perceptive than those who left, more sophisticated and knowledgeable than those who left. We are the desperate people, Lord; we are the people who have come to know that we have no other option. You are the revelation. You are the Word. You have the words of eternal life, and we have believed."

As Christians today, we also have to admit that we don't have any choice. We don't have another option. There is one way to life, and we have come to know that it is Christ. "We have believed, and have come to know" (v. 69)—what an incredible statement! You see, Peter isn't stuck in Plato's cave. He has "come to know." We don't merely "have a hunch" or "feel that this is more likely than not." We don't buy into a cultural-linguistic system here, deciding that we want these words to be our words, adopting the meaning that comes in the communal apprehension of these words. Unlike Dawkins's atheist bus campaign, we don't say "probably." Instead, "We . . . have come to know, that you are the Holy One of God" (v. 69). This is not faith in faith; this is faith in Christ.

As we see from Peter, this statement is humble, yet it is very confident. This same humble confidence leads the apostle Paul to say, "Live or die, I know these things to be true. This is my confidence; I stake my life upon these truths." And he charges Christ's other followers with that humility when he says to Timothy, "Follow the pattern of the sound words that you have heard from me. . . . Guard the good deposit entrusted to you" (2 Tim. 1:13–14).

I do hope that we have a humble theology, but our humility is based on our admission that our knowledge was granted to us, revealed to us, shown to us; that we were drawn into it; that we were called out of our blindness into sight; that these truths are not only matters of intellectual apprehension but are the transforming truth that has reshaped and transformed us. We are different knowers than we were before. We are different thinkers than we were before. We are people who answer as Peter did the question, "Do you also want to go away?" We do not answer, "Lord, we are not going away, because we are more faithful, or because we love this system of truth, this tribal meaning and these words that have become so precious to us that we do not know ourselves without these words." No, there is a blessed gospel desperation in our answer. In the humility and confidence of Peter, we say, "To whom shall we go? You have the words of eternal life, and we have believed, and have come to know, that you are the Holy One of God" (John 6:68–69).

By God's grace, we are not stuck in Plato's cave. Our problem is more dire than we ever knew, but our salvation is sweeter than words can express. We preach, share, teach, and proclaim the gospel, not as those who have figured these things out on our own and are trying to help others to figure them out. Rather, we proclaim the gospel because we are aware that God still calls his people according to his pleasure and gives them to the Son. Our humility is not the humility of one who says, "I don't know," but the humility of the Christian who says, "I have been known, and now I know. And what's more, I know in whom I have believed. I am persuaded that he will accomplish all that he has said until that day."

10

I Am the Truth

D. A. CARSON

FROM THE BEGINNING of Genesis to the beginning of the gospel of John, the power of the word of God for creation and many other things is demonstrated. The Bible itself, as the Word of God, gives us a foundational understanding of the Christian faith. However, the Word of God is not pertinent only to those things outside of us—the world we live in, the Word we read and study and learn from. Rather, a common theme in Scripture is the importance of the Word to what happens *to* us as believers: the process of sanctification. Even in light of the great comforts and joys that we can glean from the Word of God, its role in our sanctification lends our "knowledge of the truth" great practical importance.

The theme of "knowing the truth" through Scripture for our sanctification is found in many places, but allow me to remind you of a handful. As early as the Pentateuch, in Deuteronomy 17, Moses anticipates the importance of the Word to kingly rule. Centuries before a king takes the throne of Israel,

Moses insists that the king "write for himself on a scroll a copy of this law, taken from that of the priests, who are Levites" (v. 18). ("This law" may refer to Deuteronomy or the entire Law of Moses—at any rate, its centrality is recognized even as it is being written.) The ruler is to diligently study and be absorbed in the Word of God:

> It is to be with him, and he is to read it all the days of his life so that he may learn to revere the LORD his God and follow carefully all the words of this law and these decrees and not consider himself better than his brothers and turn from the law to the right or to the left. Then he and his descendants will reign a long time over his kingdom in Israel. (Deut. 17:19–20)

In other words, when a king comes to the throne, his first task is not to audit the books of his predecessor nor to appoint a minister of war or a secretary of state. The first thing he is to do is to take out a quill pen and write out either Deuteronomy or the Pentateuch. This process is much more involved than downloading a CD onto a hard drive; rather, the king would have to write with his own hand a personal copy of the law to read every day for the rest of his life. If only these three verses of the Pentateuch had been observed, Old Testament history would have looked quite different!

Later, in a different leadership context, as Moses passes the baton of leadership to Joshua, God tells Joshua, "This book of the law shall not depart out of your mouth, but you shall meditate on it day and night. . . . Then you shall make your way prosperous, and then you shall have good success" (Josh. 1:8 RSV).

The opening lines of the Psalter echo the same message of the importance of hearing God's Word—and warn against the danger of hearing too much of the words of others. Psalm 1:1

describes what the righteous man is *not* like: "Blessed is the man who does not walk in the counsel of the wicked or stand in the way of sinners or sit in the seat of mockers." The first criterion is that he is not to pick up the counsel, the advice, or the frame of reference of wicked people. The reason is that if he were to listen long enough, he might wind up "standing in the way of sinners." Here, the Hebrew idiom does not mean what the English idiom suggests. In English, "standing in someone's way" involves blocking their path. You might picture Robin Hood or Little John standing on the bridge so that travelers would end up in the stream. However, in Hebrew, "standing in someone's way" means "doing what they would do." In English, we might say "walking in their moccasins." So if you follow the advice or counsel of wicked people, soon your lifestyle will be indistinguishable from theirs: you now stand where they stand and do what they do, for you "walk in their way." And if you do that long enough, you may wind up "sitting in the seat of mockers." Now, instead of merely indulging in wicked ways, you begin to look down your long, self-righteous nose at those stupid, bigoted, conservative Christians and, with sneering condescension, mock them. At this point, Spurgeon says, those who do this "have taken their degree in vice, and as true Doctors of Damnation they are installed."[1]

On the other hand, Psalm 1:2 describes what the righteous man is like and lists only one criterion: "His delight is in the law of the Lord, and on his law he meditates day and night." In other words, over against the advice of wicked people stands the advice of God. The righteous man does not simply have his devotions quickly before he beats it out the back door on his way to work—"Gotta get this over with again." No, God's Word is his delight; he turns it over in his head and meditates

1. C. H. Spurgeon, *The Treasury of David: Containing an Original Exposition of the Book of Psalms*, vol. 1, *Psalm I to XXVI* (London: Passmore and Alabaster, 1870), 2.

on it. If he wakes up in the middle of the night, that's where his mind goes. And, if God's Word really is his delight, if that's what he's thinking about, if that's where he is getting his advice, then it will shape his life and his attitude. He will be, as verse 3 metaphorically describes it, "like a tree planted by streams of water, which yields its fruit in season and whose leaf does not wither. Whatever he does prospers." This is not a picture of a coniferous tree compared with a deciduous one, as we might think in our temperate North American climate. The psalmist was envisioning a different comparison. This tree was not planted near a wadi, the sort of stream that is full during the early rains and then is dry and dead until the later rains fall. No, the Word of God comes as life-giving water with a constant supply. The hearer of God's Word is planted by a confluence of streams, such that there are always signs of life. His leaf never, ever withers, and in due season there is fruit.

Throughout the Old Testament, we read of the Word changing a person's thinking and resulting in godly living. In Jeremiah 17:8, we find a similar description of a thriving tree. More explicitly, Proverbs 23:7 states, "As [a man] thinks in his heart, so is he" (NKJV). And the New Testament is full of this theme as well—for example, Romans 12:2: "Be transformed by the renewing of your mind." So when Jesus speaks in John 17 of the role of the Word in sanctification, he is summarizing the whole force of Scripture.

The Bible's message that "You are what you think" and its image of life-giving streams ring a bell for someone like me, who grew up in French Canada on the shores of the dirtiest river in Quebec. In those days, folks were less concerned about pollution, and there were three pulp mills upstream. In the summer, when the river went down, it stank. We still drank from it, of course, because they dumped in tons of chlorine, so you either smelled the dirty river or you smelled the chlorine. These habits were challenged later in my boyhood, when one of the bottled water companies invaded our territory and in both French and English plastered our town with their slogan: "You are what you drink." But the Bible probes even more deeply the connection between thoughts and life-giving streams: "Guard your heart, for it is the wellspring of life" (Prov. 4:23).

At this point, we must make a second observation about the role of the Word in sanctification. It is important to note how God's Word does *not* sanctify us. Sanctification by the Word does not come about by mere education, by compartmentalizing it in our lives, by sheer magic, or by mere proclamation. These misconceptions run rampant in our society, but they are not the truth that sets us free.

First, knowledge of the Word does not sanctify us by mere education. I have now lived long enough and have belonged to enough professional biblical societies that there are not many front-rank New Testament scholars in the world whom I have not met. Some of them are very brilliant minds indeed. One chap in Germany used to conduct a postdoctoral seminar in which he wanted only a few people, the brightest of the bright. So on the first day, he offered them a test: write out the epistle to the Ephesians in Greek. Well, that got rid of a lot of the less determined, but there were still too many students for the professor's preference, so the next class was another test: write out the epistle to the Ephesians in Greek and include the apparatus. If you know Greek, you understand how terrifying that sort of assignment would be, and you know how skilled and brilliant the students that completed the course must have been. But that knowledge is not the sanctifying work of the Word.

When I first went to England in 1972, Professor C. H. Dodd was still alive. He was one of the last of the old-time polite, pious liberals, and he had a massive knowledge. When he was about ninety, a BBC radio interviewer asked him an intriguing question: "What if, by some fluke, every copy of the Greek New Testament were destroyed? How much of it could you reconstruct?" Professor Dodd replied, "All of it." His mastery of the scriptural text was impressive, but that knowledge is not the sanctifying work of the Word.

In fact, some very technically competent New Testament scholars are self-professed atheists. Many deny supernaturalism or are no more than deists. But they know their text.

Admittedly, even within a confessional evangelical framework, it is possible to think somehow that because we're spending time studying biblical texts, we're becoming more holy. But you don't have to spend too long at a seminary before you realize that sometimes studying all those texts may make you unholy. A certain kind of a pride may set in, or you fall into the routine of just meeting another deadline or taking another quiz. You find yourself studying the New Testament as if you were studying microbiology or nuclear physics or Shakespeare. Mere education does not guarantee anything. Abstracted from the power and unction of the Spirit of God, a kind of idolatry of learning can appear, even in the scholarly work of believers. Such learning of the text does not guarantee the sanctifying work of the Word.

Neither does learning the Word lead to sanctification if it "remains upstairs," to use the language of Francis Schaeffer. Schaeffer distinguished between "upstairs thinking" and "downstairs thinking,"[2] noting that it's possible to learn the text and be pious at a remote "upstairs" level, but it's not affecting whom you're sleeping with. It's not affecting what you do with your

2. See, for example, Francis A. Schaeffer, *He Is There and He Is Not Silent* (1972; repr., Wheaton, IL: Tyndale, 2001), 41.

money. It's not affecting how you treat your spouse. Downstairs, where you actually live, it's not changing very much.

This reality challenges a saying that is wonderful and often true—but, unfortunately, not always. I have written this quote, which is often attributed to Jonathan Edwards, on the flyleaf of my own Bible: "This book will keep me from sin, or sin will keep me from this book." But that saying is not absolutely true. It is possible to keep studying "this book" to finish an exam, to write another book, to finish your exposition, to finish your sermon preparation, to prepare for the Sunday school class, to seem faithful in having your devotions so you can say you've had your devotions—and still to sin like a trooper. Some of us have worked with ministers who have been powerful in the Word, seen people genuinely converted, and watched their ministries expand, only to get exposed in a double life that has gone on for years and years. It's a matter of "upstairs/downstairs" thinking.

This reality can be illustrated by the tragic case of a friend of mine a few years ago. After his wife found out that he had been leading a secret life, she listened to him preach for an entire summer before the situation blew up in public. He preached spectacularly good sermons, even at weddings that he was conducting. So she said to him, "How can you say these things when you're not living that way yourself?" And he answered, "I'm a professional." His life goes to show that, no, the Word does not sanctify us by remaining upstairs.

Third, the Word does not sanctify us by mere magic. I do not know what else to call this category. Here I am talking about an approach to pietism and to piety that may not always be as crass as to say, "A verse a day keeps the Devil away," but that somehow still suggests that memorizing a few verses or reading the Bible is like rubbing Aladdin's lamp: you get God on site, and blessings come along. It's a kind of pious approach to the

Bible. These people may not know the Bible very well, but they thumb through its pages, looking for little gems of blessing.

A verse sometimes adduced to justify this kind of unrooted, unanchored approach to the Bible is John 20:29. After Thomas has confessed, "My Lord and my God!" (v. 28), Jesus responds, "Because you have seen me, you have believed; blessed are those who have not seen and yet have believed" (v. 29). Our culture often interprets this to mean that, although Thomas's faith was grounded in reality, it's actually better to believe without any evidence, without being grounded in anything. "Blessed are those who have not seen and yet have just taken my word for it—that's a better kind of faith." But that is not what this passage means. Such an interpretation results from imposing on the text some frames of reference, with respect to the Christian faith, that are astonishingly recent in conception.

To comprehend why this kind of misconception is so foreign and new to Christianity, one must understand that history itself is an essential part of understanding Christian faith. Any comparison of world religions underscores this importance. Go to Thailand. Befriend a friendly neighborhood Buddhist and ask in fluent Thai, "Suppose you could prove that Gautama the Buddha never lived. Would that knowledge destroy Buddhism?" The answer would be, "Of course not." No element of Buddhism depends on any proposition about the historicity of Gautama's life. Buddhism depends for its credibility on its internal coherence, on its attractiveness as a system. It does not depend on any historical truth claim.

Now go to India. Suppose you could prove beyond any shadow of a doubt that the god Krishna never existed. Would you destroy Hinduism? Of course not. Hinduism has millions of gods; no one even knows them all. Hinduism is part of a cyclical system of karma, in which the aim is to rise or fall within the system of reality, hopefully in progressive cycles upward until you are absorbed in truth itself and come to deepest consciousness and awareness (nirvana). Getting rid of a god or two would not affect the structure of things too much.

Or talk to your neighborhood Muslim imam and ask, "Could Allah have given his final revelation to someone other than Mohammed?" Now, your neighborhood imam might initially misunderstand your question. But the question is not whether or not Muslims think that the final and greatest revelation went to Mohammed. The question is, "Could Allah, had he chosen, have given the final revelation to somebody else?" The answer is, "Well, of course." A Muslim's historical claim is that Allah did give this final revelation to Mohammed, but the revelation doesn't depend on anything intrinsic to Mohammed's life. The history of Islam could have looked much different without threatening its major claims.

But now, turn to your neighborhood pastor. Could God have given his final revelation to someone other than Jesus? In a Christian frame of reference, the question doesn't even make sense, because Jesus *is* the revelation. If you could prove that Jesus never lived, you would utterly and completely destroy every vestige of biblical Christian faith. We not only claim the finality in Jesus that the Muslims assert with respect to Mohammed. We make a whole series of historical claims about Jesus. He was God incarnate, seen and touched and handled. He died and rose again. In his resurrection body, he ate fish and was seen; his wounds were touched. There was continuity between the body that went into the grave and the body that came out. The historicity of all this is key. Paul reminded the Corinthians, "If Christ has not been raised, your faith is futile . . . [and you] are to be pitied more than all men" (1 Cor. 15:17, 19). There would be nothing left to proclaim.

In John 20, Thomas has to be convinced that Jesus rose from the dead, and when he is convinced he bows before Christ and says, "My Lord and my God!" By doing so, Thomas becomes one of the links in the necessary historical chain. With the other apostles, he sees, touches, and eats with this resurrected Christ. Jesus knows that after them will come a vast number of men and women, drawn from every tongue and tribe and nation, who will not see the resurrected Christ, who will not see in order to believe until Christ himself comes back. Yet they will believe—and not as the Buddhists, Hindus, and Muslims believe. On what basis will they believe? They will believe on the basis of the historical witness of that first group. Blessed is the vast number who will not see, but will come to faith because Thomas bore witness at that point in time. The author of John reports that "Jesus did many other miraculous signs in the presence of his disciples, which are not recorded in this book" (John 20:30)—that is, other miraculous signs in addition to the resurrection and the ones already recorded. These historical records are necessary, he says, "that you may believe that Jesus is the Christ, the Son of God, and that by believing you may have life in his name" (v. 31).

Therefore, biblical Christianity does not simply turn on "a verse a day to keep the Devil away," a little bit of piety, a little bit of encouragement. It turns on something massive: God's becoming a human being in space-time history, God's disclosing himself, God's sending his Son to "[bear] our sins in his body on the tree" (1 Peter 2:24). It depends on the historical reality of God's bearing the curse, God's sending his son to avert his own just wrath, so that we might be "accepted in the beloved" (Eph. 1:6 KJV). It depends on God's raising Jesus from the dead and on God's sending Jesus to be the conquering king, fighting all battles until the last enemy, death, is destroyed (1 Cor. 15:26) and the entire universe is handed over to the Father. That historical time line is biblical Christianity.

As we describe ways in which the Word does *not* sanctify us, let me go one stage farther: knowing the truth does not sanctify us by mere proclamation. I know that it's God's purpose to save men and women by the gospel preached. But we sometimes have the impression that, provided we preach well, speak the truth, and are faithful, results will follow. But, of course, Jesus provides a contrary example. As he said, "Because I tell the truth, you do not believe me" (John 8:45). Notice that he does not say, "*Although* I tell the truth." That would be bad enough. But it's "*because* I tell the truth." In other words, it's the truth itself which guarantees that these people will not believe. So what was Jesus supposed to do? Should he have started shaping the truth so that people would be more likely to believe? What do you do when it is precisely the articulation of the truth—of forceful, powerful, intelligent, Spirit-anointed, unction-filled truth—that is causing the unbelief?

Jesus is not the only example of this pattern. Isaiah's preaching was doomed, as well. "In the year that King Uzziah died," Isaiah "saw the Lord . . . high and lifted up" (Isa. 6:1 ESV), just as God was asking in the counsels of heaven, "Whom shall I send?" (v. 8). And Isaiah put up his hand and said, "Please, please may I go?" Having been terrified in God's holy presence and realizing how wonderful his forgiveness and purification were, Isaiah wanted to speak as a mouthpiece for God. But listen to God's reply: "Go and tell this people: 'Be ever hearing, but never understanding; be ever seeing, but never perceiving.' Make the heart of this people calloused" (vv. 9–10). By speaking truth, guarantee their callousness. Because of the truth, they will reject you. And Isaiah said, "For how long, Lord? I mean, I don't mind doing it for ten years, even twenty years, if then we'll have revival." But that is not what happened. God told Isaiah to keep preaching the Word faithfully until the entire nation was under attack from the armies of foreign nations. When, finally, only ten percent of the nation was left, God would cut it down until there was only a stump in the land. Only at that point does God give the first glimmer of hope: that out of the stump, a new shoot will come (v. 13). But the shoot of Jesse wouldn't appear until seven hundred years later, well after Isaiah's lifetime. All of his truth-speaking ministry was guaranteed to be a public failure.

So we must not delude ourselves into thinking that, just because we're preaching faithfully and truly, we are guaranteed certain results. At the end of the day, it takes the Spirit of God to open up hearts and minds. Some of us will be called to ministries in parts of the world that are astonishingly fruitful, and others will be called to ministries in parts of the world that are astonishingly tough. Do you really think that missionaries in South Korea are godlier than those in Japan? Do you think that missionaries sent to Latin America, who have seen so much fruit, are godlier than those who slip into the countries around the Persian Gulf?

It's important to be realistic about all the ways in which the truth of God's Word does *not* sanctify us. It does not sanctify us by mere education, by remaining upstairs, by mere magic, or even by mere proclamation. Only the transforming, enlightening, converting, life-giving power of the Spirit of God changes lives.

So we come to our third point: God's Word *does* sanctify us by driving us to Jesus—Jesus Christ crucified, risen, and coming again. The gospels move us toward Jesus Christ and Jesus Christ alone. What is required of us, empowered by the Spirit, is the differential between those who truly believe and those who don't.

To reinforce this, let's look again at John 8:30: "Even as [Jesus] spoke, many put their faith in him." But at the same time, some "put their faith in Jesus," but were not really saved. According to John 2:24, for example, Jesus did not commit himself to many of those who had put their faith in him, because he knew what was in the human heart. He didn't need anybody to tell him that these people's hearts were corrupt and deceitful and that their allegiance wasn't for real. That's why, in John 8:31–32, he says to the Jews who had put their faith in him, "If you hold to my teaching, you are really my disciples. Then you will know the truth, and the truth will set you free." There is a propositional kind of believing. Even the Devil himself believes that Jesus rose from the dead (James 2:19). But it is holding to Jesus' teaching, abiding in it, that actually opens up the epistemological doors—the kind of obedience that finds Jesus saying, "Then you will know the truth, and the truth will set you free."

Now there is a lot of preaching today that misses this point. In preaching the Gospels, many basically present a series of psychological profiles about how people act on faith. For example, in the feeding of the five thousand, much can be made of the fact that the disciples themselves didn't have any clue what to do. Their advice was, "Let's send them off to town so they can buy food. How can we feed this lot?" But one little boy with five loaves and two fishes gave the little bit that he had, and, because he offered what he had, all of the others were fed. Isn't Jesus wonderful for multiplying the little bit that we give him?

Well, there's some truth to that. But the purpose of the Gospels is not to give us a psychological profile of how we might share our lunches. It's not even to give us a psychological profile of how people come to faith. In fact, even coming to faith in the Gospels is a bit different from the way we come to faith today. Let me give you an example. In Matthew 16:15, Jesus asks the disciples, "Who do you say I am?" and Peter responds, "You are the Christ, the Son of the living God" (v. 16). Jesus frankly acknowledges that Peter received this understanding as a gift from the Father (v. 17).

But Peter's understanding of who the Christ is was not quite the same as yours and mine. When you and I confess that Jesus is the Christ, we automatically include in this confession the understanding that he died on the cross and rose again on the third day. Peter obviously did not understand that truth, because when Jesus began to talk about how the Son of Man was going to Jerusalem to be crucified and on the third day rise again, Peter immediately said, "Never, Lord! . . . This shall never happen to you!" (v. 22). From Peter's point of view, messiahs win; they don't lose—especially one like Jesus, with all those miracles. Peter was waiting for an anointed king in the line of David who would triumph. Clearly, his understanding of the Messiah, though true, was still only partial and so deeply defective that Jesus said, "Get behind me, Satan! You . . . do not have in mind the things of God" (v. 23).

Now, this passage does teach that we come to acknowledge the truth precisely as a gift from God. But that is not the whole point. The Gospels are designed to drive us toward an understanding of who Jesus is, why he came, and what he does—and along the way, we happen to pick up other lessons about how to share your lunch or that true understanding comes as a gift from God. These are important lessons to learn, but the dominant truth of the Gospels is the grace of God and the person and work of his dear Son, who goes to the cross as a ransom for many and rises from the dead for their justification. In our reading of Scripture, far from merely focusing on one little passage that gives us a pious thought for the day, we must always be thinking of how each verse fits, not only into the immediate four-gospel story line, but into the entire biblical story line. Then we will begin to see God's unfolding purposes and learn how to read the entire Bible in a grace-centered, Christ-centered, cross-centered way.

Many people have come to a genuine knowledge of Jesus Christ, and have put their faith in him. But it's possible to have a good understanding of the gospel, and then almost feel it slipping away through our fingers as we reach to pat ourselves on the back about that gospel knowledge. We start with our good understanding of the gospel—understanding in truth that we are accepted before God, not because of our genes or ethnicity, education or money, or anything other than the sufficient merit of Jesus Christ, who died on our behalf. We understand that, live that, rejoice in it. But then we think, "I wonder if God will bless me today, because I didn't spend much time on my devotions. My prayer life is a bit short. Will God be mad at me?" On the other hand, if we have a wonderful day of devotions, do we think, "Well, God is bound to bless me today"? We may never be quite so crass as to put it this way, but don't you almost feel the gospel slipping away from you there?

We misuse the Word of God and lose our sense of the gospel. So it's not too surprising that when young people come through our churches with all kinds of physical, social, and academic expectations on them, they then go off to university, where most of our young women suffer from bulimia, anorexia, or dependence on Prozac, because they can't live up to all the standards imposed on them by themselves, their culture, and their parents. What would even begin to meet that need but the grace of God? Many of our young guys avoid any sense of responsibility or wisdom via a narcissism that keeps them from growing up until they're over the age of 28. Even then, some can't make up their minds, because they are always looking over their shoulder to see if something better is coming along. What our world so desperately needs is men and women so transformed by the gospel in the Word of God that their acceptance—in their own minds, before brothers and sisters in Christ, and before God—is not bound up in anything other than the grace of God.

Finally, once the life-giving Word of God sanctifies us as God's truth rightly learned and applied, this Word shapes our worldview. Here we turn to the contributions of biblical theology (through which you follow the Bible's story line all the way through) and systematic theology (through which you ask questions like "What is God like?" "What is sin?" and "What did Christ do?"). Both disciplines are desperately needed for establishing a frame of reference for our thinking. One thing our Bible reading must teach us is the categories of Scripture as they run through the Bible: concepts such as covenant, temple, priesthood, sacrifice, rest, reconciliation, imputation, faith, church, and so on. Then, if you encounter any one of them and remember how they work, lights blink on and you see what God is doing.

Let me give you an example by sketching out the high points of the temple time line throughout Scripture and how it can illuminate our reading of a particular passage. If you are reading Ezekiel, eventually (after the wheels in wheels and judgment everywhere) you encounter a spectacular vision in chapters 8–11. Ezekiel is transported seven hundred miles away from the banks of the Kebar River to see all of the idolatry in Jerusalem and the glory over the temple somehow moving with the mobile throne-chariot. It's a fascinating image. But if you place this passage on the axis of the temple story, it becomes simply profound.

There are intimations of "temple" already in Genesis, but let's begin tracing the tabernacle from the time of the giving of the law, when God specified exactly how his dwelling place was to be built. More than thirty times in Exodus, God reminds them to be sure to build it according to the pattern he showed Moses on the mount—with its Holy Place and the bread of presentation, the curtain, and the Most Holy Place behind the curtain, where even the high priest could go only once a year, carrying blood to pay for his own sins and those of the people.

Once it was built, the glory of God hovered over that tent. Then, in due course, the glory would lift and go off, and the tabernacle was just a tent again. So the Levites could pack it up and carry it on their shoulders until the glory would hover again. The people would stop at a new place, set up the tent, and the glory came down. The glory-cloud pointed to God's presence at this great meeting place between God and human beings. God ordained where people were to come before him with fear and the knowledge that cleanliness could be obtained only before this God by the sacrifices that he himself had ordained.

Eventually Solomon built a permanent temple, and when the glory came on the temple, all the Levites and priests scattered. The glory was so overwhelming that they could not stay in the temple. In that time of great dedication, Solomon prayed, "The heavens, even the highest heavens, cannot contain you. How much less this temple I have built!" (2 Chron. 6:18). Yet it was still the place where sinners met God.

But in Ezekiel's vision, the Lord shows him that the city of Jerusalem is now so foul, so rebellious, so idolatrous, that it will be destroyed—even the city of the dynasty of the great king David, the city of messianic promise, the city of the temple. The people in Jerusalem don't want to believe it; the people in exile also don't want to believe it, because then there would be no home to return to. But in this spectacular vision, Ezekiel sees the glory of God abandoning the temple and perching itself on this mobile throne-chariot that leaves the city, crosses the Kidron Valley, and goes up on the Mount of Olives. Ezekiel comes back out of his vision and tells all this to the people in exile. He says, "Don't you understand? If Nebuchadnezzar destroys the city, it's not because

God is not strong enough. It's not because the Babylonian gods are more powerful. It's because God has abandoned the city in judicial wrath; the temple is now only masonry."

Our understanding of the temple story line provides a context that renders the image of God abandoning Jerusalem powerful. This image then informs our understanding of the rest of the temple story line in Scripture. It highlights the significance of God's statement to the people in exile, seven hundred miles away from Jerusalem, "I will be a sanctuary for you" (see Ezek. 11:16). However important the temple is, however important the sacrificial system is, where God is determines where the temple is.

It also grants new meaning to our postexilic tracing of "temple." Eventually the people do come back in small numbers and another temple is built—but the kingdom is never restored to its former glory. We can trace the theme of "temple" through the prophecies of Haggai and the reformation of Nehemiah until one day, in the streets of Jerusalem, a voice is heard saying, "Destroy this temple, and I will raise it again in three days" (John 2:19). Because we understand the biblical background of "temple," we can infer that he wasn't talking about masonry. He was saying that he is the great meeting place between God and human beings, not just by virtue of his incarnation but also by virtue of his destruction. In the New Testament, the antitypes of the temple, the great meeting place between God and human beings, are identified variously as Jesus, or (in Paul's writing, predominantly) the church, or (in one or two places) the individual Christian's body. We collectively and individually are the temple of the living God, the meeting place between God and the broader world. This view forms the foundation of all evangelism.

Finally we come to the Book of Revelation, and the use of "temple" language changes again. We see that the New Jerusalem is built like a cube. Have you ever imagined a city looking like a cube? But there is only one cube described in the Old Testament—you're supposed to pick up on it—the Most Holy Place of the tabernacle and the temple. The point now is that the city embracing all the people of God is always and forever in the presence of God, without any veil or mediating priest, for in that city we worship him who sits on the throne: "I did not see a temple in the city, because the Lord God Almighty and the Lamb are its temple" (Rev. 21:22).

Now, I've sketched out only one story line found in Scripture. There are dozens of other lines of thought to trace in biblical theology. Noting them helps you to piece your understanding of the whole Bible together. As a result, whenever you're reading, you pick up these things and see how they come together, and then you fall down and worship because you're playing out the whole story line in your mind as you're reading through and meditating on the Word. It will not do to avoid using biblical categories. The same principle applies to understanding different literary genres—the different ways God has disclosed himself: in lament, in exaltation, in wisdom literature, in oracle, in prophecy, in typology. God has given us this rich Word that captures us and takes us on, doing so on every front—literary, typological, dramatic, historical—bringing us to Jesus again and again, until our minds are captured by God, who gave us Holy Scripture, and his dear Son, whom he sent to redeem us.

Above all, sanctification by the Word involves holistic thinking under the shaping authority of revelation, so that the truths of Scripture become impressed on our understanding, our consciousness, our categories, until we look at the whole world differently. For instance, there is a fundamental difference between secular psychologies and a truly biblical psychology. It's a fundamentally different view of human beings. If you have an anti-supernatural worldview, or you don't have a category for sin that sees the human heart in rebellion against God, all your psychological remedies are inevitably going to be different. Common grace may lead you to insights, but at the end of the day, a biblical worldview will shape how you think about right and wrong, about who people are, about what's still to come, about whether your expectations rest on who wins the next election or on the Jesus who will receive the kingdom of this world on the last day.

Until your Bible reading moves you in that direction, it is too small, too narrow, merely empty magic. Pray that the Holy Spirit of God will so embed his truths in your heart and your life that his Word will not simply be information but will be truly transformative—the power of God unto salvation to those who believe.

ALLIANCE®
OF CONFESSING EVANGELICALS.

What is the Alliance?

The Alliance of Confessing Evangelicals is a coalition of pastors, scholars, and churchmen who hold to the historic creeds and confessions of the Reformed faith and who proclaim biblical doctrine in order to foster a Reformed awakening in today's church. Our members join for gospel proclamation, biblically sound doctrine, fostering of reformation, and the glory of God. We work and serve the church through media, events, and publishing.

The work started in media: *The Bible Study Hour* with James Boice, *Every Last Word* featuring Philip Ryken, *Mortification of Spin* with Carl Trueman and Todd Pruitt, *No Falling Word* with Liam Goligher, and *Dr. Barnhouse & the Bible* with Donald Barnhouse. These broadcasts air throughout North America as well as online at AllianceNet.org.

PlaceforTruth.org is our online magazine—a free, "go-to" theological resource. ChristwardCollective.org is a theological conversation equipping believers for growth. And reformation21.org provides cultural and church criticism. Our online daily devotionals include *Think and Act Biblically* and *Making God's Word Plain*, as well as MatthewHenry.org, a resource fostering biblical prayer.

Our events include the Philadelphia Conference on Reformed Theology, the oldest continuing national Reformed conference in North America, and regional events including theology and Bible conferences. Pastors' events, such as reformation societies, continue to encourage, embolden, and equip church leaders in pursuit of reformation in the church.

Alliance publishing includes books from trustworthy authors, with titles such as *Zeal for Godliness*, *Our Creed*, and more. We offer a vast list of affordable booklets, as well as e-books such as *Learning to Think Biblically* and *How to Live a Holy Life*. And we encourage sound biblical doctrine by offering a wide variety of CD and MP3 resources.